Antique Furniture Repairs

Antique Furniture Repairs

Charles H. Hayward

Evans Brothers Limited

Published by Evans Brothers Limited
Montague House, Russell Square,
London, W.C.1.

First published 1967

This edition completely revised and reset
© Evans Brothers Limited 1976
Third printing 1981

Set in 9 on 10 point Univers by
Photoprint Plates Limited, Rayleigh, Essex
and Printed in Great Britain by
Hazell Watson & Viney Ltd, Aylesbury, Bucks

ISBN 0 237 44831 9   PRA 7125

Contents

Woodworkers' Conversion Tables

Imperial inches	Metric millimetres	Woodworkers' parlance (mm.)	Metric millimetres	Imperial inches	Woodworkers' parlance (in.)
$\frac{1}{32}$	0·8	1 bare	1	0·039	$\frac{1}{16}$ bare
$\frac{1}{16}$	1·6	$1\frac{1}{2}$	2	0·078	$\frac{1}{16}$ full
$\frac{1}{8}$	3·2	3 full	3	0·118	$\frac{1}{8}$ bare
$\frac{3}{16}$	4·8	5 bare	4	0·157	$\frac{5}{32}$
$\frac{1}{4}$	6·4	$6\frac{1}{2}$	5	0·196	$\frac{3}{16}$ full
$\frac{5}{16}$	7·9	8 bare	6	0·236	$\frac{1}{4}$ bare
$\frac{3}{8}$	9·5	$9\frac{1}{2}$	7	0·275	$\frac{1}{4}$ full
$\frac{7}{16}$	11·1	11 full	8	0·314	$\frac{5}{16}$
$\frac{1}{2}$	12·7	$12\frac{1}{2}$ full	9	0·353	$\frac{3}{8}$ bare
$\frac{9}{16}$	14·3	$14\frac{1}{2}$ bare	10	0·393	$\frac{3}{8}$ full
$\frac{5}{8}$	15·9	16 bare	20	0·787	$\frac{13}{16}$ bare
$\frac{11}{16}$	17·5	$17\frac{1}{2}$	30	1·181	$1\frac{3}{16}$
$\frac{3}{4}$	19·1	19 full	40	1·574	$1\frac{9}{16}$ full
$\frac{13}{16}$	20·6	$20\frac{1}{2}$	50	1·968	$1\frac{15}{16}$ full
$\frac{7}{8}$	22·2	22 full	60	2·362	$2\frac{3}{8}$ bare
$\frac{15}{16}$	23·8	24 bare	70	2·755	$2\frac{3}{4}$
1	25·4	$25\frac{1}{2}$	80	3·148	$3\frac{1}{8}$ full
2	50·8	51 bare	90	3·542	$3\frac{9}{16}$ bare
3	76·2	76 full	100	3·936	$3\frac{15}{16}$
4	101·4	$101\frac{1}{2}$	150	5·904	$5\frac{15}{16}$ bare
5	127·0	127	200	7·872	$7\frac{7}{8}$
6	152·4	$152\frac{1}{2}$	300	11·808	$11\frac{13}{16}$
7	177·5	178 bare	400	15·744	$15\frac{3}{4}$
8	203·2	203 full	500	19·680	$19\frac{11}{16}$
9	228·6	$228\frac{1}{2}$	600	23·616	$23\frac{5}{8}$ bare
10	254·0	254	700	27·552	$27\frac{9}{16}$
11	279·5	$279\frac{1}{2}$	800	31·488	$31\frac{1}{2}$
12	304·8	305 bare	900	35·424	$35\frac{7}{16}$
18	457·2	457 full	1,000	39·360	$39\frac{3}{8}$ bare
24	609·6	$609\frac{1}{2}$			
36	914·4	$914\frac{1}{2}$			

Note
The imperial and metric sizes given for tools and joint parts etc. cannot work out exact, but providing one works to one or the other there is no difficulty. In the timber trade it is accepted that 1 in. = 25 mm.

Walnut veneered clothes press with superficial damage easily put right. Note the missing pieces of half-round moulding (cross-grained) around the drawers. Photograph by courtesy of Collins Antiques, Wheathampstead, Herts.

Foreword

It follows as a natural sequence that the popularity of antique furniture has brought into being the trade of the furniture restorer. Just as the production of motor cars has made inevitable the car repairer, so the skill of the restorer has followed that of the furniture maker. Indeed, the two trades have something in common in that, the older the item, the more attention it is likely to need. Furthermore, although a second-hand car at first becomes reduced in value with every passing year, it does eventually become a vintage car, when its value begins to rise again. So with furniture, mere second-hand being of little value until it has acquired the respectability of age, and then becomes a thing of worth. It is usually reckoned that a hundred years is the minimum for an antique (though the car can scarcely claim this), and so it is that every year sees the emergence of respectable old furniture which had previously been the doubtful stock-in-trade of the second-hand dealer.

My own connection with restoration began before the war of 1914. Our workshop made a speciality of antique repair work, and we had a warehouse full of old woodwork in various stages of decrepitude, from bundles of broken legs and rails (which were once chairs) to sideboards and tables, etc. with smashed legs or loose frames, ancient sections of panelling, dusty scraps of worm-eaten carved oak, and a curious collection of oddments that were no longer identifiable. One by one, these rickety pieces would be brought out to be made good, and were periodically replaced by other oddments bought at sales. There was thus a constant flow of work, some of the items emerging much as when they were brought in except for being mended, others being converted into more salable or more profitable pieces, or cannibalized to patch up other things, parts of which had been lost.

In addition, furniture belonging to customers came in for repair from time to time, and sometimes some curious alterations had to be made to meet some special requirements of the customer (I once had to convert a dining chair into a night commode). Nearly all the items came in for re-polishing, and sometimes this amounted almost to vandalism when, say, a table top had its polish scraped off merely to remove a few scratches. With the scraping went the finish built up by years of patient polishing with wax, plus the faded colour, the result of exposure to light over the years. Today we have realized the folly of this, but at that time the application of bright French polish was thought more of than the patina built up over the years.

Of all the items to be repaired, chairs were one of the most exacting, because they came in for more use (and abuse) than any other piece of furniture, and because they had to withstand the weight of a person and the movement inevitable with their use. Frequently half a dozen would come in for repair, the main trouble being loose or broken joints, and I recall the test made by the foreman after mending. Planting one knee on the seat, he would rock the back first one side, then the other, and if it stood up to this it was satisfactory—as indeed it should, for the force he used was almost enough to break a new chair. By and large they survived the test, though on more than one occasion I have seen a joint crack—sometimes in an entirely new place.

Occasionally a repair would be almost impossible, or so expensive as to be impracticable, and such jobs were known as 'breakers'. These, according to the particular fault, were either converted into something else or were used merely for their old wood and were built into other items. Such things were kept in the warehouse until a use in another connection occurred. There must be any number of pieces in existence which began life in another and possibly less exalted form. Generally, such conversions were reasonably successful, but occasionally they looked as though they had had an uneasy birth of doubtful parentage.

The necessity for skilled repair work is realized today, and there are in fact institutions which specialize in courses for training purely in the restoration of old pieces. The majority of people doing this work are basically cabinet-makers because they have the necessary skill in using woodworking tools, and are (or should be) familiar with methods of construction in solid wood as distinct from plywood, laminboard, etc. This is a matter of considerable importance, because failure to realize and accept the fundamental fact that solid timber is liable to shrink as it dries or swell if it becomes damp, can result in future trouble. For many years woodworkers have known this elementary fact, and have evolved methods of construction which allow for movement yet give reliable, strong construction. Much modern furniture consists of man-made materials which are practically inert so that movement need not be taken into account.

Yet, although a man may have been a cabinet-maker turning out new pieces of furniture, he finds himself confronted with entirely new problems when he has to tackle repair work. In the first place the repair must be unobtrusive, if not invisible; much of the old wood has to be retained; and it must enable the piece to face years of further service. Then there is the practical difficulty of having to carry out what may seem a minor operation without dismantling other parts of the job. Furthermore, it may be extremely difficult to apply cramps or other means of holding the work together.

When the job was first made, there were probably special cramping portions (especially in shaped work) which were cut away after completion. The repairer has to do without these. Special parts such as inlay bandings, etc. may not be available, and the repairer will have to make them personally to replace missing parts. The same applies to lost portions of carving.

Old nails and screws are almost inevitable, and they can appear in the most unlikely places. In fact, the experienced repairer comes to regard them almost as a sort of by-product of wood. They are bad enough when whole, but frequently they have broken off short and remain embedded in the wood. Their removal may be essential, yet it has to be done without leaving unsightly gashes. The question of colour and finish is also important and, although some large repair shops employ polishers who specialize in finishing only, the repairer in a small shop frequently has to do his own finishing.

Another consideration is that of dealing with worm-eaten wood. It has to be made safe against further damage, yet has to be strong enough for further service. The idea that all old, infected wood must be cut away is not viable—it might involve cutting away nearly the whole job! Sometimes a part may be nothing more than a shell (especially one of walnut), the surface almost perfect, yet riddled inside with worm tunnels, so that it could be crushed by gripping with the hand.

Restoration seldom stays at repairing old furniture, however, at any rate in the trade. Sooner or later left-over oddments become part of something else or are converted into more valuable items, and it calls for the judgement of Solomon to decide whether the job is purely a fake or is something which has been given a new lease of life and would otherwise have become useless. Sometimes it is done in an entirely innocent way, someone merely having oddments of woodwork to be converted into something useful. I recall being asked by a customer to make a large standing cupboard from oddments of oak panelling and the result was a quite successful job in which all the parts were old and of a period. It made a useful piece, but was not a *genuine* cupboard. That had been constructed some fifty or so years ago, and quite likely the then owner has long ceased to have any use for a cupboard, old or faked. Presumably it is still about somewhere, and owned by people happy in the delusion that they possess a genuine seventeenth-century cupboard.

Taken all round, the work of repairing antique and old furniture calls for rather special requirements, patience being an outstanding one because much of the work is anything but straightforward. No two jobs are ever exactly alike, and at the end there s often little to show for the work involved (at any ate when the job has been well done) because he repair has to be invisible or nearly so, whereas a man making a new piece has the job itself to show for his labour.

Yet, all things considered, it is rewarding to be able to put back into service a thing which would otherwise be fit merely for the scrap-heap, or at least to save it from further deterioration. Faults in old furniture are largely progressive in that one trouble will quickly lead to another if neglected, so that the last state of the item is worse than the first. Certainly, restoration is a highly skilled job, as one soon comes to realize, for quite often a lot of time has to be spent in putting right a botched repair that an unskilled man has done previously.

Although I have ceased to do practical restoration, I still look back on the earlier years in the workshop with feelings of nostalgia; the crisp sound of shavings curling from the plane, the sight of beautifully figured veneer, the scent of newly sawn wood, and even the eternal smell of the glue pot. I suppose that it lies in human nature to remember the pleasant side of things and forget the rest. Experience seems to glow with the false radiance that leaves the seamy side in shadow, yet I really believe that my years in the workshop were amongst the best I have spent in my working life. Whether I would want to start all over again is another matter.

The author wishes to thank those who have been kind enough to allow photographs to be taken in their workshops, and in particular F. G. and C. Collins, Wheathampstead, Hertfordshire. Also those who have supplied photographs of items repaired in their workshops.

Charles H. Hayward, St Albans   1975

The oak plinth removed, the ground-work beneath made good where decayed, and the veneer cut back to a clean line.

The three photographs on this page were taken in the workshops of COSIRA and are of special interest in that they show the restoration of the base of a grandfather clock case which had suffered badly as a result of a previous unskilful repair.

(above left) The base of the clock case as it arrived in the workshop showing how an oak plinth, completely out of style, had been mitred round apparently to make good some decayed and worm-eaten wood.

(below left) The completed restoration. The veneer has been replaced where missing, and a new, walnut-veneered plinth added with cross-grained moulding at the top edge.

Chapter one

Principles of Restoration

Although there are a few cases in which an item is in a really bad way, yet has to be preserved for exhibition in a museum, most old furniture is expected to go back into service and withstand the everyday usage that this entails. It follows, then, that a repair must be strong as well as look right. If this sounds a little obvious, it is as well to reflect that it is often simpler merely to re-glue a breakage just as it is than to strengthen it by some internal means such as a dowel or other stiffener. Gluing parts only necessitates holding them together whilst the glue sets, but it is quite another matter to insert dowels in the correct position so that the parts go together in alignment.

I have seen it stated that a repair should leave the job as strong as when in its original condition, but I doubt the accuracy of this. Most breakages leave a weakness and, when it has been neglected for some time before repair, the parts become worn and loose, and for this reason alone the job cannot be as strong as when originally made. Yet a repair must be reasonably strong. A dining chair, for instance, must be capable of being used for general purposes, though it is unreasonable to expect it to stand up to being tilted backwards on its back legs, or to withstand the abuse of parlour tricks. In the same way, a carcase must be rigid, or a drawer remain sound when filled with goods and subjected to everyday use.

Apart from strength, however, a repair must be unobtrusive, if not invisible. There are occasions when the line of a breakage in the nature of things is bound to show, but it should not unduly proclaim itself. And this brings us straight away to the question of how far one should go in renovating an old piece, also whether the replacement of missing parts should be disguised or left as obviously later additions. Taking the last point first, there is probably some merit in leaving the new parts clearly for what they are when the item is in a museum where it will be studied for its period, though it is to be admitted that many such exhibits have had later additions which have either been

Fig. 1 (left) Bureau needing extensive repairs. Although the main carcase is reasonably sound, the moving parts are in a bad way. The fall is damaged at the corners: also the lopers. All drawer bottoms are split, sides are badly worn, and all joints need re-gluing.

antiqued or have become old and worn in themselves as a consequence of subsequent usage. Probably most of these additions were made at a period long before they found their way into the museum.

On the other hand, when an antique has to come in for a further period of use in the home, there seems no point in advertizing the repairs, especially when there is no doubt about the detail of the replacement. For instance if, say, a shaped bracket is missing, and there are other corresponding brackets, the new one can be a literal copy of the others, and it can be stained and finished to match the rest of the job. This cannot be classed as faking; it is rather making the piece fit to live with, for to leave it frankly new is to make it glaringly obvious. In the same way, repairs to inlay bandings which have chipped away in parts should be made to tone as closely with the old as possible.

So far as the extent to which repairs should be carried out, it is generally a matter of considering each case on its merits. Broken structural parts must be made good, and that as soon as possible after breakage. Otherwise additional strain may be thrown on other members causing these to fail also. Similarly, missing mouldings should be replaced, and when, say, a corner has been badly smashed it needs to be made good. On the other hand, a corner which has merely become rounded with use should be left as it is. It is largely a matter of common sense.

Veneers call for special consideration. Chipped or missing parts need replacing, and the repair should be done in the most unnoticeable way. Bubbles must be pressed down, and other blemishes dealt with as far as practicable, but cases do sometimes occur when nothing short of complete replacement is of any use. For example, I once had to repair a table which was originally veneered with burr walnut. It had apparently at some time been left in the damp so that much of it had lifted and there were almost as many gaps as veneer. To attempt a repair would have left it more like a patchwork quilt, and the whole thing was replaced. When, however, the veneer has merely come away and is

otherwise sound, it can usually be lifted and re-glued in place. In fact, this operation is sometimes necessary when groundwork joints have failed

Marquetry repairs can be extremely expensive when damage is extensive. In fact, the cost may be so high as to make it impracticable.

Perhaps the biggest problem is that of replacing parts when there is no means of knowing what the originals were like. It calls for considerable knowledge of period styles plus good taste. Otherwise an anachronism may easily occur—as indeed one often finds in old pieces. Usually the safest way is to look up photographs of similar items to see the detail. Probably the exact part will not be found but it is usually possible to adapt the form to the job in hand.

One point which holds good no matter what the defect may be is to do the repair as soon as possible after the breakage. There are several reasons for this. Firstly, the failure of one part often throws extra strain on others so that these in turn begin to suffer. Thus a chair leg which has become loose involves movement in adjoining parts causing other joints to fail.

Secondly, broken-off parts have a habit of disappearing, and it is therefore better to re-fix them whilst they are still available. Furthermore, when parts are first broken the edges are sharp and clean and they can be put back in the most unnoticeable way. When left off for any length of time the corners become rounded over and worn, so that a really clean join becomes impossible. Moreover, the constant cleaning and handling results in furniture cream or grease finding its way on to surfaces which have to be glued, and all of this has to be removed if the glue is to do its work properly

Lastly, it is nearly always advisable to complete all structural repairs before dealing with small decorative detail. There is the odd occasion when, say, a loose rail has some detail in it which is more conveniently put right before it is re-fixed in position, but generally it is safer to make sure the job is rigid first.

Chapter two

The Repairer's Workshop

A fairly large work area is desirable, if not essential. Apart from the space needed for the bench, tool chest and trestles, etc., room is needed for the jobs themselves in various stages of dismemberment. A chest of drawers, for instance, occupies double its normal space when all the drawers are taken out, and the room needed for gluing up can be quite considerable. A garage is frequently used by the small repairer (providing it is not needed for a car), but if it is in permanent use for repairs a wood floor is highly desirable. Reasonable light is essential and there should be some means of warmth because, apart from personal comfort, it is invariably necessary to warm joints before assembly (when Scotch glue is used), and it is almost impossible to assemble a large job in a cold shop in winter-time. The glue would chill too quickly. Furthermore, when the job comes to be finished any polish would be liable to turn milky-white with damp and cold.

The bench itself can be the normal woodworker's type with head vice, though the German bench with additional tail vice has its advantages. The tools needed are basically those of the cabinet-maker with a few extra items for the special problems inherent in repair work. Many of these extra tools or appliances are made by the repairer himself (some of them cannot be bought), and for this reason no two of them are ever exactly alike. Some of them are nothing more than normal tools which are too worn out for ordinary use, but which are good enough when the presence of nails, etc. is suspected. The following is a list of the extra items which are worth having.

A Hacksaw. Apart from cutting metal fittings, screws, etc., this is invaluable for sawing wood in which the presence of nails is suspected.
B Drawer runner saw. For cutting in grooves in worn drawer runners (see also page 22).
C Drawer runner router. Used in combination with the above (see also page 23).
D Upholstery springs. For holding parts of irregular or awkward shape whilst glue sets.

(left) Typical furniture repairer's workshop. Although the usual kit of cabinet-makers' tools is needed, special appliances are also required to deal with individual problems. The repairer usually makes these up for himself. (Workshop of Charles Brown, West Wycombe.)

15

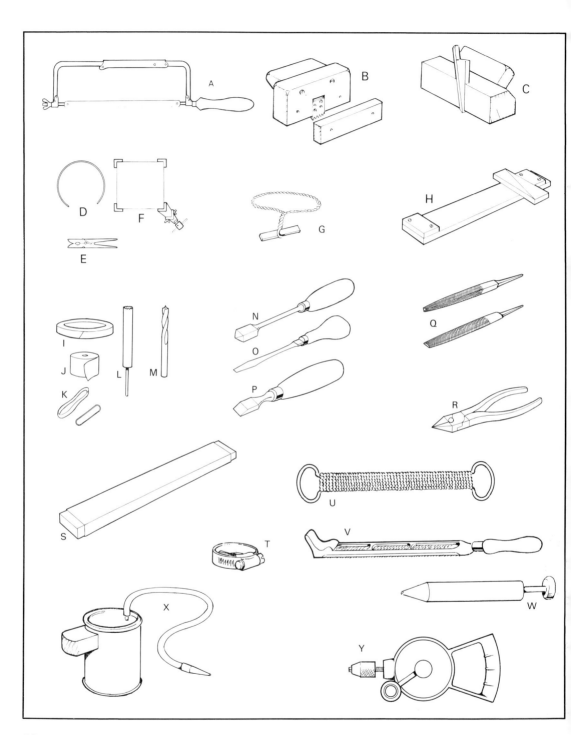

Springs are cut to any convenient length. Two or more can be linked together.

E Spring clothes pegs. For light pressure on mouldings, etc. whilst glue sets.

F Wire cramp. Often useful on chairs and similar frames when several joints have to be glued simultaneously, or when there are rounded corners which would be awkward for cramps.

G Tourniquet. Rope or cord, for similar purposes to above.

H Folding wedges. Used with bars of various lengths when sash cramps are impracticable or not available.

I Gummed Tape. To hold veneer to prevent joints from opening as moisture dries out, and to hold items of irregular shape whilst glue sets. Also pressure-sensitive tape used to hold items of irregular shape when being glued. No dampness needed. It grips purely by pressure of the fingers (see also page 59).

J Self-adhesive tape. The transparent type often handy because of its immediate adhesion.

K Rubber rings. For odd shapes needing light pressure only. Cross-cuts of old motor tyre tubes are often useful.

L Broken screw borer. To remove a rusted screw which cannot be withdrawn by other means. Used in the brace. The toothed edge cuts around the screw (see also page 33).

M Morse drills. Used in wood in which old nails are likely to be encountered. Note the special grinding.

N Soldering iron. To apply heat locally to veneered surface to take out bubbles, or when taking out bruises by damping and heating.

O Old screwdrivers. Not for withdrawing screws, but for levering items apart, punching old fittings, etc.

P Old chisels. For scraping old glue or dirty parts, or for any purpose for which one would hesitate to use a good chisel.

Q Files. Often needed to trim old fittings, cut through metal parts, etc.

R Pliers. If ground to special shape at the nose, useful to extract nails flush with surface.

S Cloth pads. Pair invariably required on which to place furniture with polished surface whilst repairing.

T Jubilee clips. Useful to bind the ends of turned legs whilst gluing or boring.

U Burnisher. For rounding over edges and simulating the effects of wear.

V Shapers. For the rapid reduction of wood. Often better than rasp or file as they are non-clogging. Various kinds available, flat, rounded and rat-tail.

W Glue pump. For introducing glue into a joint that cannot be separated. It is generally necessary to bore a hole in the wood.

X Steam applicator. To soften glue in an otherwise firm joint. Made from tin with tight-fitting lid. A long rubber pipe is fitted over a soldered-in tube and the other end fitted with a nozzle. A hole is bored in the wood to receive the latter.

Y Drill. Used for pre-boring nails in wood which would otherwise be liable to split. Sometimes a nail or needle can be filed to form a suitable drill.

In finishing materials the repairer needs a variety of substances including water stains, various chemicals, French polish, dry powder pigments, fillers, wax, candle grease (for lubrication), fine canvas for strengthening thin cabinet backs, drawer bottoms, etc.

Chapter three

General Carcase Repairs

These are largely structural, and include the carcases of wardrobes, sideboards and similar items. Mostly they are dovetailed together, though not invariably. The general principle to be followed is not to separate parts unnecessarily. With really loose joints there is no option, but it should be remembered that taking glued items apart always loosens the joints, dovetails in particular. Furthermore, a certain amount of violence is usually necessary, and this may result in further damage being done. When a carcase is reasonably rigid there is little purpose in knocking it apart, especially when there is a firm back to prevent racking. In any case, quite a lot of work is involved in complete dismantling. It is not merely the work in knocking apart and re-gluing, but also that of getting rid of all dried-up glue. Furthermore, it often happens that the process causes other things to

Fig. 1 Eighteenth-century bureau, modernized in Victorian times and badly in need of repair.

Fig. 2 The bureau in **Fig. 1** after restoration and removal of Victorian knobs and turned feet.

Fig. 1

Fig. 2

become loose, so that instead of a straightforward operation, other repairs may be involved. The principle then is to let well alone.

Dismantling. When this is unavoidable I have always found it a time-saver to mark the parts so that they can be replaced in the correct positions with certainty. Do not strike the wood directly with hammer or mallet. Apart from bruising the surface the blow is purely local and will most likely crack the wood or cause a joint to fail. Instead, place a stout batten across the wood up to the adjoining part and strike this as in Fig. 3. In this way the force of the blow is spread over the width, so minimizing any splitting tendency, and the batten takes the hammer marks. Make sure beforehand that nothing else is holding the parts together. There might be a rail, back, pilaster, or what you will, screwed to both parts and this would prevent them from separating. Make sure, too, that there are no nails or screws driven in. This may have been done in earlier repairs in an attempt to stiffen the whole. One other point to be reckoned with is the order in which the parts are taken apart. It is quite possible that one member cannot be released until another has been taken out. Sometimes, too, one part locks another in position, and it may be necessary to cut this before it can be shifted. This, incidentally, is another reason why unnecessary dismantling is avoided.

The separating of obstinate dovetails can sometimes be helped by putting a damp rag over them and heating with a flat iron.

Making Good. The parts being separated, it is worth considering whether any local repairs are best done before the parts are re-assembled. It sometimes happens that a small repair can be done more easily on the bench. In any case, it is necessary to get rid of all dried-up glue. Sometimes a swab or small brush dampened with hot water can be used for the purpose, but as a rule scraping with a chisel or knife is necessary. In any case, do not flood water on to the joint as it may easily cause the wood to swell. If any rubbed joints have failed it is essential to plane them afresh and, since this inevitably makes the wood narrower, it needs to be done carefully with as few shavings as possible. Short joints can be planed dead true, but in the case of long wood

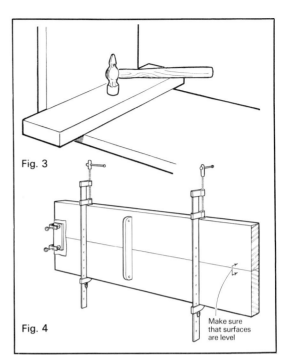

Fig. 3

Fig. 4

Make sure that surfaces are level

Fig. 3 Separating carcase parts. Batten avoids bruising and spreads force of blow.

Fig. 4 Re-gluing a rubbed joint. The thumbscrews at the end ensure the surface being flush. Alignment is tested by the straight-edge.

plane the joint slightly hollow and put on one cramp in the middle, or two spaced along the length as in Fig. 4. This ensures that the ends, always the most vulnerable parts, are held tightly together. Test to see that the parts are in alignment and are level, because the original surface has to be retained, and no subsequent levelling is possible.

All being ready, the job can be re-assembled, this being done in the reverse order from knocking apart. As a rule cramping is needed even on dovetailed joints because the separating invariably loosens them. Battens should be placed across the job just inside the dovetails and cramps tightened over these as in Fig. 5. Often the cramps need also to be put along the direction of the dovetail owing to the loosening, and possibly to

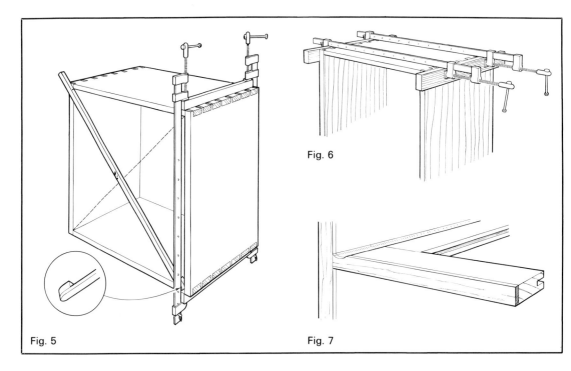

Fig. 5

Fig. 6

Fig. 7

Fig. 5 Cramping a carcase with through dovetails. Note that the battens are placed just inside the dovetails. Squareness is tested by means of the diagonal rod.

Fig. 6 Cramping carcase top in direction of dovetails. This is frequently necessary when dovetails have become slack. Note use of battens over the laps.

Fig. 7 Badly worn drawer rail and runner. In this case the rail is softwood with hardwood facing.

correct any distortion of the ends. Fig. 6 shows the idea. The pressure of the laps of the pins against the ends of the tails will hold the top and bottom, though it may be necessary to tap them down after the cramps have been put on.

Assuming that Scotch glue is used, heat the parts thoroughly beforehand, as glue chilled on cold wood loses much of its grip. Generally assistance is desirable, especially on a big job. Test for squareness before setting aside for the glue to harden. Generally the diagonal rod is the most

satisfactory method as shown in Fig. 5. This should register the same length when reversed into the opposing corners. The inset drawing shows the pointed end of the diagonal rod with its applied facing piece. This drops into the corner leaving the main rod on the face.

Test also to see that the carcase is free from winding. Stand it on a flat floor free from any oddments of wood, and look across the edges from the side. Any winding will be obvious at once. Glue which has squeezed out can be removed when half set with a chisel, but do not leave until it has completely hardened. Where surfaces have been polished the glue will not adhere.

Drawer rails. These have their own particular problems. The chief fault found is that of extensive wear at the sides where the lower edges of the drawers rub. Often the rails are of softwood faced with hardwood at the front, or just veneered. With continuous use over the years the ends of the rails are scored into a trough, as in Fig. 7. I have had cases in which the rails have worn to less than half their original thickness. The drawers themselves are invariably correspondingly worn at the back, but the repair of these is dealt with in Chapter eight. Wear spreads, of course, to the runners, and these have either to be made good or entirely replaced.

Fig. 8 shows a satisfactory method of repairing the fault. First the runner is removed. It is usually held at the back with a screw, the front being stub-tenoned into the back of the rail. As a rule it rests in a groove across the end, just the front being glued, and it is simple to undo the screw and prise the runner out from the back. A saw cut is made across the top of the rail well to the outside of the worn part and the area chiselled away flat. It helps if an undercut is made in the chest, this not reaching to the front but set in about 6mm. ($\frac{1}{4}$in.). The new patch is correspondingly bevelled at the end so that it can be pressed in and lowered into position. It will invariably give enough to be sprung in. Sometimes it is better to cut just into the rail tenons which are necessarily partly exposed.

The new patch should be full at the front so that after the glue has set the edge can be levelled. Following this the facing can be cut well back at an angle and a new patch of the same kind of wood glued in. This again is full at the edges and is levelled after the glue has set.

Alternative method. Another method sometimes to be preferred when the wear is slight is that in Fig. 9. In this the upper face of the rail is sawn across at an angle both in width and depth, and the waste chiselled away. The new patch is of the same wood as the facing and is inserted from the front. The undercutting prevents any lift at the inner side, and the plan angle enables the patch to be fitted easily since it is quite loose until right home when a tap from the front makes it tight. It should be held with a cramp when being glued.

Note that both sides are full so that they can be levelled afterwards. The new runner is planed to a good fit in the groove, and its inner edge is grooved to hold the dustboard. It fits with a stub-tenon into the groove in the rail. At the back it is either sawn off at an angle to simplify screwing or is notched. Make the clearance hole generous so that the runner does not resist shrinkage of the end. When fixing, glue the tenon and first 25mm.

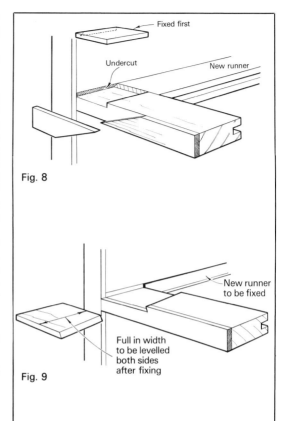

Fig. 8

Fig. 9

Fig. 8 Repair to worn drawer rail. The old, worn runner is replaced. It is usually stub-tenoned into the rail.

Fig. 9 Alternative form of repair to worn drawer rail. The tapered shape ensures a tight fit when the piece is tapped home.

(1in.) or so of the runner, leaving the rest dry so that it does not resist movement.

A more awkward repair is when the rails take the form of partitions of solid wood running from front to back without separate runners, Fig. 10. The wear is chiefly on the front third or half, and it is necessary to cut grooves so that replacement pieces can be glued in. The awkward part is in cutting the groove because it is right up against the end which makes sawing difficult, and prevents the ordinary router from being used.

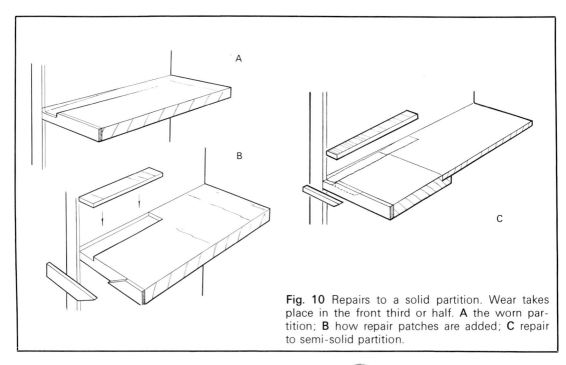

Fig. 10 Repairs to a solid partition. Wear takes place in the front third or half. **A** the worn partition; **B** how repair patches are added; **C** repair to semi-solid partition.

Personally I use the simple gadgets shown in Figs. 11–14. That in Fig. 11 is for cutting down the side of the groove immediately against the carcase end. It is a block of wood about 127mm. (5in.) long by 50mm. (2in.) deep and 21mm. ($\frac{7}{8}$in.) thick. At one side a saw-like cutter is inset flush, and held with two screws, the latter being countersunk flush. Its projection at the sole can be varied to suit the depth required by having staggered holes as in Fig. 13, and entering the screws in holes which give the required projection. To the other side of the block is screwed a strip of wood flush at the bottom with the main block, its purpose being to act as a depth stop by bearing against the unworn part of the partition. Above it is fixed a handle (see also Fig. 12). In use it is worked back and forth, the side with the cutter kept hard against the end of the carcase. To

Fig. 11

Fig. 11 (above right) Drawer runner or partition saw. As arranged here it is used for the side nearest the chest end.

Fig. 12 (below right) The runner saw as set up for the side away from the chest end.

Fig. 12

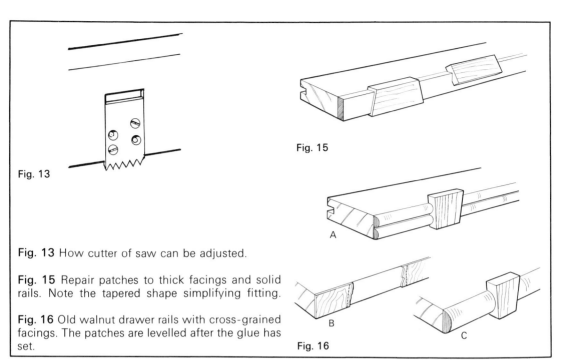

Fig. 13

Fig. 15

A

B

C

Fig. 16

Fig. 13 How cutter of saw can be adjusted.

Fig. 15 Repair patches to thick facings and solid rails. Note the tapered shape simplifying fitting.

Fig. 16 Old walnut drawer rails with cross-grained facings. The patches are levelled after the glue has set.

cut the other side of the groove both depth stop and handle are removed and fixed to the other side as in Fig. 12, and used as before, hard against the carcase end.

Much of the waste can be chiselled away, but to bring the groove to even depth throughout, the second tool shown in Fig. 14 is used. Any plough cutter about 6mm.–9mm. ($\frac{1}{4}$in.–$\frac{3}{8}$in.) wide can be used. It is fixed at a fairly steep angle and is held by a wedge as shown. Note that the front of the latter is sloped at a slight angle so that there is no liability for either wedge or cutter to slip outwards. The projection of the cutter, equals the required depth of groove.

The groove being cut as at Fig. 10B, the new piece of wood can be glued in. It is seldom necessary for it to go back farther than from one-half to two-thirds the depth. Cramping is usually awkward and the simplest way is to nail the slip, leaving the nails projecting, and withdraw them when the glue has set. Note from B how the front edging is cut back and a new piece of hardwood fixed. Repairs to thick facings and

Fig. 14 Router used to finish groove in drawer partition.

solid hardwood rails are shown in Fig. 15. Note that the sloping ends are not only neater but are easier to fit, because once the correct angle has been cut it is only necessary to push the part in to make a tight fit.

In old walnut furniture the drawer rails were frequently made of softwood or oak with a cross-grained veneer at the edge as at Fig. 16B. This simply calls for cutting away the fractured veneer ends to a sharp line, cleaning away the old glue and rubbing down a new piece of veneer, also cross-grained, with the cross peen of the hammer. One difficulty is that old veneer was invariably thick, being cut by hand with the saw, and it is difficult to obtain such thick veneer today, most present-day veneers being knife-cut and much thinner. The only way is to follow the old-time cabinet-maker and saw the veneer from a solid block. Only small pieces are needed, and these are easily sawn. Use wood of similar grain as far as possible. Sometimes two thicknesses of knife-cut veneer can be used.

Alternatives often found in the same period of walnut furniture are cross-grained mouldings as at Fig. 16A and C. Such mouldings are invariably thin because they have to be quite elastic to avoid joints opening up due to shrinkage. It is a matter once again of cutting with a keen chisel and letting in new pieces. It is an advantage to let the ends slightly converge and cut the new piece to correspond, as this can then be pushed to a tight fit. Do not force too hard or the adjoining mouldings may break away. Fig. 17 shows part of a walnut chest with part moulded and part veneered facing needing repair.

Usually the patches required are quite short and pieces of cross-grained stuff can be glued as in Fig. 16. Occasionally a long length may be required, however, and it is awkward to handle so long a length of cross-grained wood, and in any case it would be difficult or impossible to obtain wood wide enough to enable the length to be worked. My own plan is to cut out several strips of cross-grained stuff and rub-joint them to obtain the length needed. When set, one side is levelled and veneered as at Fig. 18A, the grain of the veneer running along the length. It is then reversed and the moulding worked in the solid as at Fig. 18B. Finally, it is cut off with a fine saw, cleaned up and fitted to the chest. The veneer at the back stiffens it for handling without breaking.

Fig. 17 (above) Walnut chest of drawers with veneered and moulded rail facings needing repair.

Fig. 18 How moulded, cross-grained facing is prepared in a single length. The back is veneered as at A, and the moulding then worked, B.

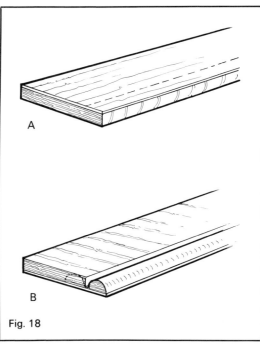

A

B

Fig. 18

The photograph in Fig. 19 exemplifies the surprises that turn up from time to time in old furniture. It will be seen that the cocked bead is worked in the facing of the carcase and the drawer rails, rather than around the edges of the drawers. As so much of the facing is missing, it would pay to prepare lengths of it as in Fig. 20 and cut it to fit. As, however, there might be quite appreciable variation in the existing facing it would be as well to work the beads slightly full in width to enable them to be levelled flush at each side afterwards.

Incidentally, the photograph in Fig. 19 shows the bare-faced dovetail joint of the rail to the ends. Assuming that it is undesirable to take the whole thing to pieces, it would certainly be necessary to work fresh glue into the joints as far as practicable. This can usually be done by a sort of pump action with the fingers, brushing in glue and working the fingers across and up-and-down over the joint.

Split ends. Not all antique and old furniture was well-made. Some of it was fundamentally unsound, and the result shows itself when pieces come into the shop for repair. One of the chief faults was that of a solid piece of wood such as a cornice moulding being planted across the grain of a cabinet. When the latter was relatively shallow, no great harm was done, especially when the wood was of a reliable type and was dry before being used. The trouble comes in a deep cabinet such as that at Fig. 21. Since the moulding is rigidly glued to the ends it resists the shrinking tendency of the ends and, as nothing can stop wood from shrinking when moisture dries out, a split is bound to occur or joints are pulled apart. Such troubles were minimized when a well-seasoned hardwood was used, such as Cuban mahogany, but there was always the risk of trouble.

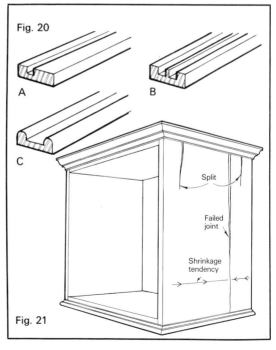

Fig. 20

A

B

C

Fig. 21

Split

Failed joint

Shrinkage tendency

Fig. 19 (above) Unusual detail in a mahogany chest. The cocked bead is applied to the ends and drawer rails rather than to the drawers.

Fig. 20 Stages in working the cocked bead detail on the chest shown in Fig. 19.

Fig. 21 Repair to a solid carcase end with failed joints and splits.

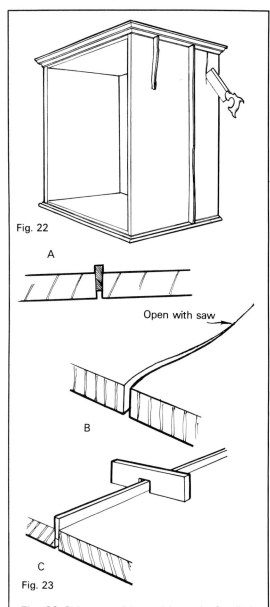

Fig. 22

A

Open with saw

B

C

Fig. 23

Fig. 22 Shivers and how thin end of split is opened.

Fig. 23 A wedge-shaped sliver glued in; B crack following the grain; C testing levelness of surfaces at each end of the shivers.

When such a job comes in for repair it can usually be assumed that no further shrinkage will occur unless it has been out in the damp. It is, therefore, a case of making good the splits or open joints. The last-named are always straight, and as a rule are parallel or nearly so. The best plan is to clean out the opening as best one can, to get rid of dirt and grease, using an old saw, thin coarse file, or anything similar. A strip of wood slightly thicker than the opening is prepared, tapered in its length if necessary if the opening is not quite parallel. It is planed to a slight wedge shape in its thickness so that it enters the opening comfortably in its length, and is glued in. It should be tapped in and left slightly proud of the surface as at Fig. 23A.

A split in the wood invariably follows the grain and may be curved. Furthermore, it always tapers. To enable a shiver of wood (as it is called) to be glued in it is necessary to enlarge the width at the narrow end with the saw in Fig. 22. The shiver is tapered correspondingly and is glued in. When the glue has set the strip is levelled down, care being taken to remove as little as possible from the adjoining surfaces. Clearly it is important when gluing in the shiver to see that the wood is level at both sides as otherwise there will be a lot of levelling to do and the repair will not be neat. This is a trap in which it is easy to fall, and for my part I use the simple device at C which is a slip of wood with straight edge and notch cut in the middle. If this is bridged over the shiver any unevenness will at once be obvious.

Note that the shiver should be only slightly tapered in section. If the taper is excessive the glue will grip only near the surface.

Chapter four

Chairs

There is probably a greater variety of problems in chair repairs than in any other piece of furniture, largely owing to the many forms they take, and to the fact that a chair takes more strain than any other piece of furniture. When properly used it has to take the weight of a person, but frequently it has to withstand the strain of a person leaning back and tilting it on its back legs, not to mention the curious uses it is sometimes put to in party games, etc. Faults may vary from a simple local fracture, the breakage of arm or leg, to the loosening of some or all of the joints.

Loose joints

When only a single joint or pair of joints has given way it is often possible to put things right by re-gluing without taking the whole thing apart. It is usually advisable to avoid the last named unless all the joints are loose because further damage may easily be caused and little is gained. The re-fixing of seat rail brackets and the addition of glue blocks after local re-gluing will often make the whole quite strong. The glue will have to be inserted as best it can, and this means that the joint will have to be opened as far as possible without straining other joints unduly. Cramps are invariably necessary, and this brings us straight-way to the use of wood blocks (softening blocks as they are called) to prevent bruising of the wood and, in some cases, to ensure that pressure is applied where it is needed, or to avoid pressure on a delicate part.

The back legs are usually curved, and the softening block has to be shaped accordingly. Some of the devices that can be used are shown in Fig. 2. To tighten a cramp over the front legs usually involves the use of tapered blocks as otherwise there is risk of the outer corner being pinched so drawing the leg out of truth. Rounded corners are invariably a problem, and usually it is necessary to make hollowed blocks with notches, as at C. These are used when the whole is taken to pieces, and enable the front to be assembled. When the side rails are being put in it is necessary to have a different arrangement such as that at D, the shaped block being held with a thumbscrew. Sometimes a leg is contained between rails, and

Fig. 1 (left) Chair wreck very costly to repair.

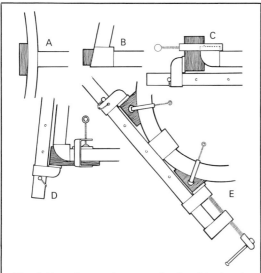

Fig. 2 Use of cramping or softening blocks. At A and B only specially shaped blocks are needed but C, D and E need to be held with thumbscrews.

then it is necessary to cramp on blocks, as at E. The actual shape depends upon the job itself, but a hole to receive a thumbscrew is often needed.

In the event of the whole not being taken to pieces but having one or more joints opened to enable glue to be inserted, a wire cramp is invaluable, as in Fig. 3. Softening pads are put beneath the corners and the screw tightened. If this is not available, use a tourniquet, Fig. 4.

Chair backs

These often present some difficult cramping problems because of the awkward shape of detail. For instance the hooped-back chair in Fig. 5 is specially tricky and often needs a large block which bridges the entire chair. Note that it clears the centre part so that the pressure is largely in line with the joints and no distortion caused. Furthermore the underside is hollowed where it touches the chair to agree with the section of the top rail. It is usually necessary to insert a piece of felt so that the polish is not marked

Fig. 3

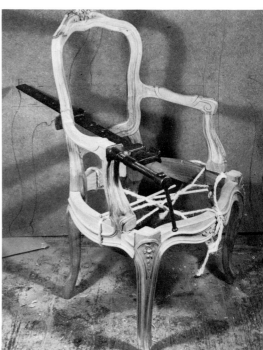

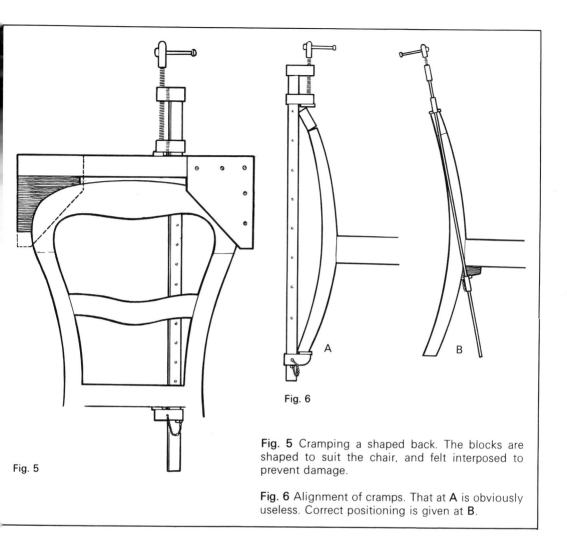

Fig. 5

Fig. 6

Fig. 5 Cramping a shaped back. The blocks are shaped to suit the chair, and felt interposed to prevent damage.

Fig. 6 Alignment of cramps. That at **A** is obviously useless. Correct positioning is given at **B**.

Fig. 3 (opp. left) Wire cramp used in chair frame. This is helpful when several joints have to be dealt with in one operation.

Fig. 4 (opp. below right) Alternative cramping with tourniquet. When ordinary cramps cannot be used owing to the awkward shape this is often useful.

Nearly every case has to be taken on its own merits. In the nature of things not only the form of chairs varies, but the type of breakage. The important thing is to exert pressure in direct line with the joint. Otherwise it will pull to one side.

In Fig. 6, for instance, it is of no use to apply a cramp as shown at A. It would only result in the rail being bent backwards. The method at B should be followed. If the seat rail is not in line with the line of pull then a temporary block must be cramped on.

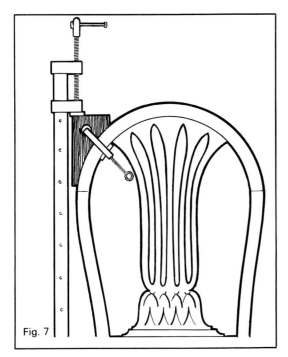

Fig. 7

Fig. 7 How hooped back is cramped.

Hooped-back chairs of the Hepplewhite type often present a problem, and the method in Fig. 7 has frequently to be followed. A block shaped to the curve is held to the rail with a thumbscrew passed through a hole and the cramp tightened over this. It is essential in such cases to make sure that the centre splat does not prevent the shoulders from pulling home. There may be old dried-up glue or dirt in the bottom of the groove, but it should be realized that the top curved rail is cut from a board which may be 229mm. (9in.) or so wide. A certain amount of shrinkage may have taken place, and this might easily prevent the main joints from pulling home. Such chairs are invariably in mahogany, however, in which the shrinkage is only slight. As the amount is only 2mm. ($\frac{1}{16}$in.) or so it is often better to take the amount from the bottom of the slat and cut back the shoulder correspondingly. The reduction is entirely unnoticeable. It is better to do this at the bottom of the slat as the shoulder is straight, whereas that at the top necessarily follows the curve of the top rail.

Missing parts

A problem that sometimes occurs is that a new member is needed to replace a broken part. When the chair can be easily dismantled there is no bother, but when the new part has to be fitted to the chair as it is there may be difficulty. Every case has to be considered individually. Sometimes there may be no option but to dismantle other parts, but it is better to avoid it when other joints are sound. A method sometimes practicable is to use loose tenons, possibly at one end only Fig. 8A shows a broken mid rail in the back. The same thing might occur in a stretcher. Having removed the broken parts they are put together as a template for cutting the new one.

Both ends are cut to receive loose tenons, though sometimes there is enough give to enable an ordinary tenon to be pressed in at one end. The loose tenon is then slipped into its mortise in the upright, and the rail, after being canted up, is lowered on to the projecting loose tenon, B A certain amount of straining is inevitable. When this is impossible, loose tenons are cut at both ends and the rail lowered on to them simultaneously.

Sometimes the joints between rails and legs are in really bad condition and merely to glue them would be of no lasting value. Usually the only way is to fit new tenons and cut the mortises back to a clean line. If the top has split (and it generally has) it is necessary to let in pieces of sound wood, as in Fig. 9. These new pieces can be rather deeper than the original set-in, and if there is a notch to receive a haunch this should be cut clean and filled in. The object is to make the top of the leg as solid and sound as possible. As a rule any new loose tenons will have to be slightly thicker than the original ones owing to the cutting away of the top of the leg.

When a new side seat rail has to be fitted note whether the back tenon is square or has to be at an angle. This happens on some chairs and a mistake is easily made.

It makes a rather stronger job if the new tenons are set down at the top, as in Fig. 10, but if the

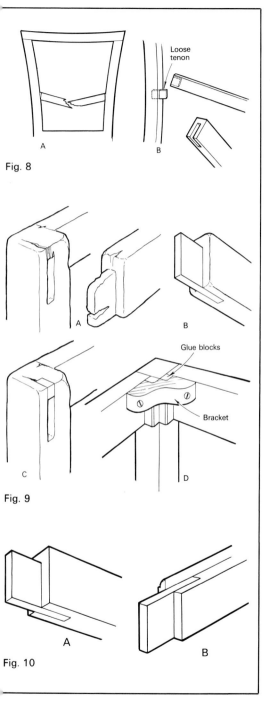

Fig. 8

Fig. 9

Fig. 10

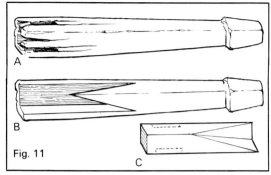

Fig. 11

Fig. 8 Replacement of mid back rail. By using loose tenons as at **B** the rail can be fixed without disturbing the main frame.

Fig. 9 Damaged seat rail joints. At **A** the mortises have split and the tenons deteriorated. New tenon is shown at **B**, and repair of mortise at **C**. Glue blocks and corner bracket is given at **D**.

Fig. 10 Loose tenons.

Fig. 11 Strong repair to a chair leg badly splintered at the top.

seat rests in a rebate at the top the slot to receive the new piece can be taken right across as the seat will conceal the joint. It is, however, stronger to stop it at the top unless it is needed to form a haunch. After gluing up, the whole should be strengthened with glue blocks rubbed in at the angles, and a large bracket glued and screwed across the rails, Fig. 9D. This can be the full depth of the rails to make a still stronger job.

A difficult case is that of a leg which has split open so badly at the mortises that any attempt to re-glue would be useless. As a rule it would be simpler to fit a new leg rather than attempt a repair, but the restorer's principle is to preserve as much as possible of the original work, and I have found the method in Fig. 11 extremely strong. Only the top splintered part of the leg is cut away at the inside, the outer surface not being affected. The leg before repair is given at A, and B shows how the top is cut away. The new spliced piece is at C. It makes a rather expensive repair, but for a valuable chair it is worth it. In this particular case the seat

31

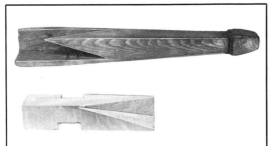

Fig. 12 View of the leg after cutting away, and the new block to be inserted.

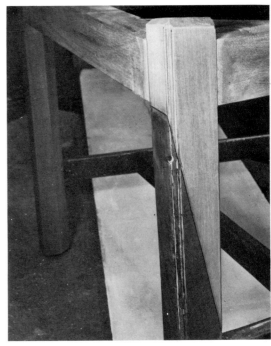

Fig. 13 The leg after the insertion of the new block.

was not of the loose drop-in type but had upholstery of the stuff-over kind.

I used the tenon saw for most of the cuts, but clearly a certain amount of cutting away with the chisel was inevitable because the saw could only be taken down as far as the diagonal. Note that the long cuts from the top of the leg align with the outer surface of the mortise, and that the sloping cuts are sawn in square with the surface. Fig. 12 shows the leg after cutting away; also the new piece of sound wood to be added. In the latter the canted cuts can be made entirely with the saw, though a certain amount of trimming with the shoulder or bullnose plane is usually necessary (if you can make these sloping cuts so accurate that no trimming is needed you are much better at using the saw than I am). As the two mortises meet in the thickness of the leg I prefer to cut them before gluing in the new piece, as it is only a matter of cross-cutting with the saw and chiselling away the waste. I generally find it advisable to cut the notches bare in depth so that there is no risk of a loose fit for the tenons. It is easy to enlarge them slightly if necessary after

gluing in the splice. Fig. 13 shows the glued-up leg ready for the projecting end to be cut off.

Another and rather simpler splice for a front leg is that in Fig. 14. The sloping cut begins immediately beneath the rails and in this way the mortises are chopped entirely in the new, sound wood.

Chairs of a later period were often dowelled together, and it is essential to remove the old dowels, clean off old glue and add new dowels. These should have a saw cut along the length to enable surplus glue to escape. Glue the dowels first to the rails, test with a pencil dropped into the holes to see that they are not too long, then glue and cramp up similarly to a tenoned job. Fig. 15 shows the joint of such a chair.

Nailed joints

One of the difficulties in dismantling old chairs is the extraordinary way in which some joints hold together. Sometimes one which seems quite

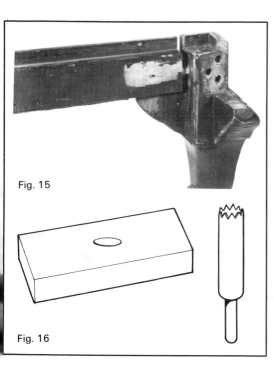

Fig. 15

Fig. 16

Fig. 14 (opp. above right) New block spliced on at top of chair front leg.

Fig. 15 Separated parts of dowelled joints.

Fig. 16 Specially-made nail or screw drill. The repairer keeps several of these in various sizes. The wood block is cramped over the nail to enable the drill to be started.

loose will resist separation. Forcible methods are often risky, especially on many eighteenth-century chairs, because they were often made in Cuban mahogany which is notoriously brittle. Often the trouble is that a nail (sometimes more than one) has been driven in in a misguided attempt to hold the parts together. Clearly the nail has to be got rid of, and this is always a problem because, to enable the head to be gripped, it is necessary to remove the wood around it, and this involves damaging the surface. Sometimes the damage can be minimized by chiselling the wood away at one side to enable a pair of side-face pliers to reach the head. However, there is no

assurance of success because often the nail has rusted in and the resistance is too great for the pliers. Sometimes, according to circumstances, it may be possible to reach the point at the other side and withdraw it that way. If the head is punched in it may cause the point to emerge at the back unless the wood is too thick. In being pulled through, the head may cause some damage, but it is invariably less than that caused by digging in to reach it.

Another method is to use a specially-made hollow drill filed from a piece of iron tube. The repairer often keeps several of these appliances in various sizes, (see Fig. 16). It is placed right over the nail head and the wood drilled away. Sometimes only a short penetration will enable pliers to be used, and in any case it will loosen part of the nail. It is invariably a case of trial and error. The rule is to cease boring as soon as the nail can be shifted. Such a circular hole has later to be filled in but it is a neater repair than chiselling away the wood. To start the drill it is usually necessary to use a block of wood with a hole in it the same size as the drill. Otherwise the latter is liable to start sideways when used. In any case it is helpful to cut in the size of the hole first with a small gouge as without this the wood is liable to be splintered away.

Loose seats

These are the easiest of upholstered chairs to deal with. In the simplest cases it is only necessary to strip off the old upholstery and replace with new. If the frame is damaged in any way, having loose joints or decayed wood, it is essential to make good. Unless the damage is trivial it is often quicker and more satisfactory to make a new frame. A badly split member can be replaced and, if the frame was originally put together with halved joints, it is easily replaced, the old part serving as a template for the new. If, however, it has mortise and tenon joints the whole will have to be taken to pieces if the tenoned member has failed. It is not worth repairing a frame in a really bad way, especially if worm-eaten, and it should be replaced, unless, possibly, it is a museum piece and there is a reason for retaining the original frame (though it may easily happen in an old chair that the frame has already been replaced).

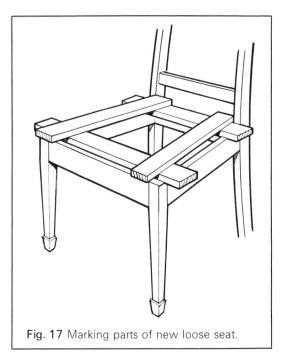

Halved joints are quite satisfactory for a seat frame if screwed and glued. The simplest way of marking the joints is to place the members in position and mark as in Fig. 17. This is more satisfactory than setting in an adjustable bevel because old chairs are frequently out of square.

After assembling and levelling the joints the edges are trimmed to leave a gap 3mm. ($\frac{1}{8}$in.) wide all round to allow space for the upholstery. All sharp edges and corners are taken off—the usual upholsterer's method is to hit the corners with the hammer. It may be, too, that the upper edges will need a fairly wide chamfer at the front and side edges if the rebate in the rails is fairly shallow. The detail in the old frames should be followed.

Occasionally one comes across some curious mistakes or skimped work in repairs. The top rail to the right in Fig. 18 is an example. At some time

Fig. 18 (below) Faulty replacement of top rail. Correct shape (though damaged) shown to the left. In that to the right the snapped-off position has never been repaired. See also Fig. 19.

the top rail has been smashed off, fracturing the wood around the mortises. Rather than make good the missing part the repairer has simply cut back the rail, re-mortised it and glued it on, adding a repair plate at the back. A correct corresponding rail is shown to the left.

A little reflection shows that the back rail was originally cut from a parallel piece of wood of width, Fig. 19B, and the correct procedure would have been to make good the missing part and cut the mortise in this. If feasible, the new block could be strengthened with fine screws. Generally one avoids metal plates in repair work when possible, but there are occasions when they are unavoidable for a chair which has to go into active use again. This may necessitate specially-made plates, particularly for parts which are frequently handled. Fig. 20 is an example. One sometimes comes across a really elaborate plate, used to strengthen the splat of a Chippendale riband-back chair in which the entire back is covered by a plate which follows the elaborate outline of the splats. Another example of specially-made repair plates is shown in Fig. 21 in which the whole of the front corner is bound by a plate and the back by a shorter one. The plates were fixed perhaps some eighty years ago by a repairer who doubted his ability to make a really strong job. They make an ugly job for they are cut right across the moulded surface.

Replacement parts

When part of a chair has to be replaced the making of the new part is simplified when the old one, even though broken, is available. It can be used as a template for cutting to shape and putting in any detail. Sometimes a corresponding opposite

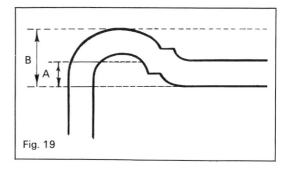

Fig. 19

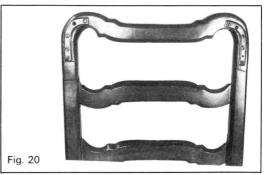

Fig. 20

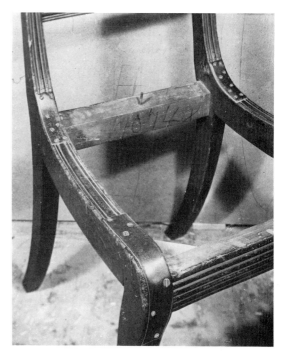

Fig. 19 Top rail of the chair given in Fig. 18. A snapped-off portion. B width of wood from which rail was cut.

Fig. 20 (centre right) Old repair plates at back of chair in Fig. 18.

Fig. 21 (bottom right) Repair plates used in an old repair. Their replacement would be expensive because the moulding has been cut away beneath the plates and has to be made good.

member can be used as in the chair in Fig. 22 in which one arm is new. Its insertion, however, may be a problem when the rest of the chair is not being dismantled. In the case of a top rail which fits over the uprights it is easy, but parts which are contained between other members can be difficult. Instances are the mid back rail, the slat, any of the seat rails or stretchers, or even a leg. Seat rails can generally be managed with care by straining the framework apart. One tenon is put into its mortise first, and the framework eased outwards until the other tenon can be slipped in. One can generally tell how far the frame can be forced without fracture.

Parts between other members, however, are much more awkward because the frame cannot be opened. It is a case of considering each repair separately. A method common in the trade is to use false tenons as in Fig. 23. The new rail is prepared and cut off to shoulder length to fit between the

Fig. 22 (left) Chair with replaced parts. The arm to the left, its support, and the left stretcher rail are all new.

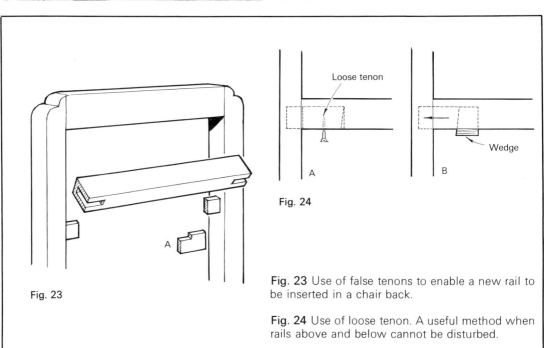

Loose tenon

A

B

Wedge

Fig. 24

Fig. 23

Fig. 23 Use of false tenons to enable a new rail to be inserted in a chair back.

Fig. 24 Use of loose tenon. A useful method when rails above and below cannot be disturbed.

uprights. Cleaning out the old mortises follows and new false tenons are glued in as shown. When the original rail has shoulders at the top edge the false tenons can be plain rectangular pieces, the open mortises in the rail being set down accordingly. If, however, the original tenons are the full width of the rail it is advisable to step the false tenons as at A so that the open mortises do not reach to the top edge where they would show.

Another method I sometimes follow is that in Fig. 24. I cut an extra deep slot in the underside of the rail and fit the loose tenon into it so that it does not project as at A. By driving a screw or nail into it as shown, it is possible to slide it back and forth. When the fit is satisfactory, it is glued and a wedge-shaped block tapped in to force the tenon home and at the same time fill in the gap. Finally the screw or nail is withdrawn.

Broken spindles such as are found in chair backs are often a problem, and the treatment usually depends upon whether the mended spindle can be replaced without difficulty, or whether it has to be inserted in a glued-up framework which cannot be dismantled. In the former case there is no special problem beyond that of making a sound repair. In Fig. 25, for instance, the broken spindle can be replaced in the framework after repair, the chair frame having been dismantled. The only point to watch is that of inserting a dowel so that the parts go together in alignment. When a lathe is available the boring is simple in that the one end can be held in the chuck and the boring bit held with its rear end against the back centre. The spindle is then revolved by hand. It is, of course, necessary to centre the bit accurately, and it is almost impossible to do this at the break because of the jagged surface. A square saw cut is therefore made at the nearest member and the short broken piece glued back in position. In this way both pieces of spindle have smooth surfaces in which the centres can be marked with gauge or dividers (see page 47), enabling the bit to be started exactly in the centre. It is then merely a matter of gluing in a dowel and cramping up afresh. It is advisable to make a saw cut along the length of the dowel to enable the surplus glue to escape, otherwise the imprisoned glue may burst open the spindle. In some delicate spindles it may be advisable to drill a small escape hole near the bottom of the dowel for the same reason.

When a lathe is not available and boring has to be done by hand, there is always the risk that the bit may be inclined to wander from true alignment with the spindle. To ensure that the parts go together straight, the method in Fig. 26 can be followed. First a means of boring accurately in the centre is needed, and a cut is therefore made at the nearest member as at Fig. 26A, and the small odd piece glued back in position at Y. A hole of the dowel size is now bored right through at X to about 25mm. (1in.) beyond the nearest convenient member, in this case Z (see Fig. 26C). It is also shown in Fig. 27. The boring should be as accurate as possible to avoid risk of emerging at the side of the spindle, and the best way, having started the hole, is to move round at right angles because it is easy to tell whether the brace leans to right or left,

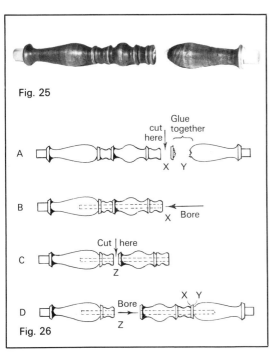

Fig. 25

A

B

C

D

Fig. 26

Fig. 25 Spindle to be repaired. In this case it can be replaced without difficulty as the framework has been dismantled.

Fig. 26 Stages in dowelling broken spindle in Fig. 25.

Fig. 27 First stage in boring the dowel hole.   Fig. 28 The spindle ready for final gluing

but more difficult to detect when it is leaning from or towards you. However, if it is a trifle out it will not matter because the hole passes beyond point Z where a saw cut is now made. Quite likely the hole revealed at Z will not be concentric (see Fig. 28), but this does not matter because the same inaccuracy occurs in both pieces and the two will go together in alignment.

The sawn-off joint at X is now glued up, and when set the bit is passed through from Z and the hole continued well beyond X. The bit is thus guided

Fig. 29 (above, centre) Broken spindle which has to be fitted to a rigid framework.

Fig. 30 (bottom) Boring the dowel hole in the lathe.

Fig. 31 (opp. above) Parts of the new centre bulb.

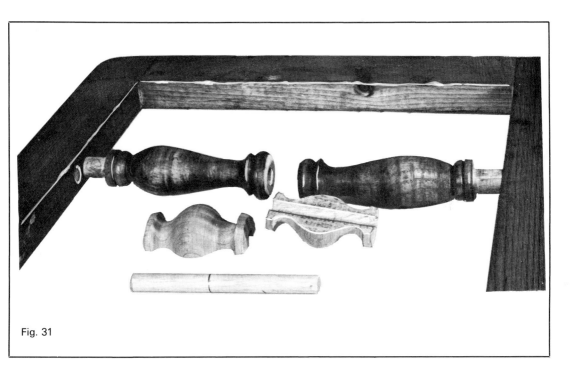

Fig. 31

and will bore accurately. Finally, the whole is glued up with a dowel rod. In the case of a very narrow spindle a steel rod of small diameter can be used.

The repair is rather more complicated when the spindle is fitted to a framework which cannot be taken apart. An example is that in Fig. 29 in which the breakage has occurred in the narrow portion of the centre bulb. The simplest way is to cut off the bulb at both ends at the side of the bead where a join will be unnoticeable. The sawn-off ends of the two side pieces are chiselled off square and the centre marked with gauge or dividers. A hole is drilled in each on the lathe as in Fig. 30, a pilot hole of about 3mm. ($\frac{1}{8}$in.) being drilled first. If the spindle is pressed backwards against the back centre there will be no danger of the bit grabbing. This is specially the case when the final size of drill is substituted.

In the one piece of spindle the hole can be about 25mm. (1in.) deep, but in the other it should be 25mm. (1in.) plus slightly more than the length of the end dowel which fits into the frame. A new centre bulb has to be turned and, as it has to be added later, it is made in two halves glued together with newspaper interposed in the joint. To make it as unobtrusive as possible, a block of wood is sawn down the middle, then glued together again with the newspaper interposed. In this way the grain matches exactly. After turning, a hole is bored through it from each end by the same method as for the end pieces. Fig. 31 shows the parts.

To assemble the whole the dowel is slipped into the deep hole and the two end dowels passed into the framework. The middle dowel can then be shifted sideways to enter the adjoining hole. The centre bulb can be knocked apart along its joint by means of a thin chisel and the paper scraped away. Finally it can be glued in position over the dowel as in Fig. 32, a cramp being applied over it.

When there is no corresponding part to use as a guide in making the replacement, it is a case of using judgement as to what it should be like. The best way is to examine other old pieces of similar date and follow or adapt the idea accordingly. An examination of photographs will often give the detail needed. Avoid an obvious anachronism.

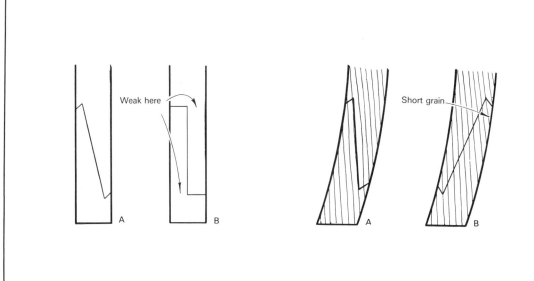

Fig. 33 Spliced joints. Stronger method is that at A, B is liable to snap off at the roots.

Fig. 34 Splices for back legs. A correct method; B faulty owing to short grain.

Legs

The repair of broken legs often calls for new pieces to be spliced on, and in the case of square sections the most satisfactory joint is tapered. A centre splice parallel with the leg is weak because it is liable to fail at the shoulders, as in Fig. 33B. The taper A has the advantage that the root of the joint is wide and therefore has maximum strength. Matters are helped, too, by hooking the ends, as in this way they resist lateral strain. In addition to gluing, the joint can be screwed if need be, the heads being counter-bored and the holes pelleted.

The new piece should be slightly proud of the surface, and when being levelled after the glue has set only a minimum of the adjoining surface should be touched. When back legs are being spliced the joint should run in the direction of the grain as far as possible as at Fig. 34A. If in the opposite direction the grain will be short and liable to snap off, B.

An unskilful repair is shown in Fig. 35. At some time the bottom of the back leg has been smashed off, and the repairer has strengthened the glued joint with screws, merely countersinking the heads. It would have been much better to counter-bore them and pellet the holes.

Another back leg repair is that in Fig. 36. The mortise had split open, but otherwise the leg was sound. Note that by sloping the ends of the patch the fitting is simplified as it is a loose fit until pressed right home. Furthermore, it is less noticeable than square-cut ends, and there is increased gluing area.

Fig. 32 (opp. above) The whole fitted to the frame-work ready for gluing.

Fig. 35 (above left) Crude repair to a back leg.

Fig. 36 (below left) Strengthening patch added at the split mortise of a back leg.

Chapter five

Chair Repairs

The photographs on the following pages have been kindly lent by the Council for Small Industries in Rural Areas, and exemplify some of the problems the restorer has to face. Some of the chairs were almost complete wrecks, and the task of repairing them called for the highest skill in putting them into usable condition. It will be seen that in many cases one of the chief causes of mischief has been the furniture beetle which has often reduced the timber to a mere shell or honeycomb. It is indeed fortunate when a chair is made of mahogany, a wood completely resistant to the pest.

Fig. 1 is a case of a Hepplewhite-style chair which has suffered badly from the beetle, the front rail being reduced to little more than a honeycomb. It will be seen that many new parts have been spliced on to strengthen the badly affected parts, Fig. 2. Without them the piece would be useless for further service. In addition are four new brackets which serve to tie together the rails and legs.

Fig. 1 (below left) Beetle-ridden chair.

Fig. 2 (below right) Chair after repair.

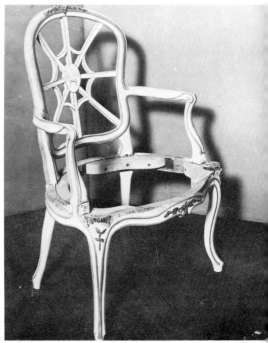

The quite frightening wreck in Fig. 3 and 4 gives a good idea of the deplorable state into which old chairs were sometimes reduced. It is French Hepplewhite in style, and fortunately is in mahogany and has therefore not suffered from the furniture beetle, at any rate so far as the show wood is concerned. It has, however, come in for some heavy maltreatment necessitating complete taking to pieces, except for the back frame. The last point is worthy of note because in most old chairs the front suffers far more than the back, the reason being that the latter forms a rigid framework with at least two horizontal rails and sometimes three. Fig. 5 shows the renovated piece.

Fig. 3 (above right) Dramatic illustration of mahogany chair which has come in for some very severe maltreatment.

Fig. 4 (below left) Photograph showing detail of leg joint to rails.

Fig. 5 (below right) Photograph of the same French Hepplewhite-style chair after extensive repair work has been completed.

In some ways Fig. 6 called for the most drastic surgery of any of the chairs in this group. As can be seen in Fig. 7, the tenons of both side rails and seat frame have been entirely eaten away. In a case like this either new pieces in which tenons could be cut would have to be spliced on, or the entire inner part of the rails would be cut away by deep sawing on the bandsaw and replaced by sound timber in which tenons could be cut. In any case shaped brackets would be glued and screwed on to tie the whole thing together. Fig. 8 shows the piece restored.

Fig. 6 (above right) Chair severely attacked by the furniture beetle.

Fig. 7 (below left) View from beneath showing how joints have been eaten away.

Fig. 8 (below right) The chair after completion of repairs.

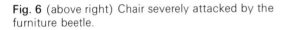

Fig. 9 is another case of a chair which has suffered from the furniture beetle. Tenons on both sides and front rails have had to be renewed, Fig. 10 and 11, and the lower portions of the back legs are entirely new pieces spliced on. Incidentally, we are asked to state that the screw holes in these back legs were not made by the restorer at COSIRA, but were the work of a previous restorer who had no confidence in his jointing and gluing. Note that the splicing of the pieces in which the new tenons of the side rails are cut avoids the removal of any show wood in the near joint, and only a minimum in the far joint.

Fig. 9 (above left) Another victim of the furniture beetle.

Fig. 10 (below left) Chair turned upside down showing back leg repairs.

Fig. 11 (below right) Woodwork repairs completed. Note new strengthening brackets.

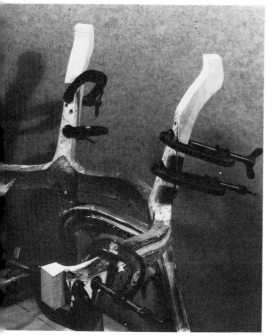

Chapter six

Various Leg Repairs

Furniture legs come in as many kinds as the types of breakages that occur. In general, however, they may be grouped under turned and square-cut, and cabriole. Each is liable to suffer from its own particular troubles, but in general it may be taken that it is usually the failure of the joints with the framework that cause the most damage. The reason is fairly clear in that mortises are invariably chopped at the top, usually on adjacent faces when the leg is at a corner (and most are). The leg is thus weakened at this point, and when any strain occurs the mortises split open. Chairs in particular suffer in this respect because of the racking strain to which they are exposed. This particular breakage is dealt with in Chapter four, Chairs. It is usually a case of making good the cracked parts and stiffening by means of brackets, glue blocks, etc.

Turned legs. Apart from the joint troubles given above, these are liable to break where one of the turned hollow members reduces the wood unduly. For instance, in Fig. 1A there is no stretcher rail to stiffen the leg, and a sudden jar at the bottom has caused the wood to fracture at the narrow part. The treatment of such a breakage depends largely upon

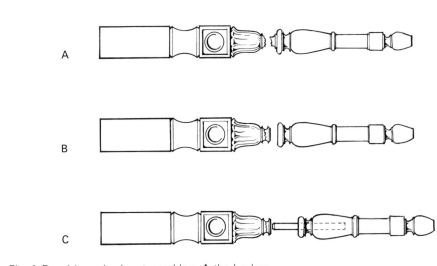

Fig. 1 Repairing a broken turned leg. A the broken leg; B leg sawn off at nearest member, and small broken piece glued on; C dowel inserted ready for assembling.

vhether the leg can be removed from the framework. When it is possible, things are simplified because the boring to receive a dowel can be done in the lathe ensuring alignment. All that is needed is to cut off the leg at the nearest member and glue the broken piece in position, Fig. 1B. This gives two flat surfaces on which centre marks can be made easily by the use of dividers or odd-leg calipers. The latter are specially useful because the curved member can be held against the side of the leg whilst the pointed leg marks the wood. By making arcs in several positions around the periphery the centre becomes obvious as in Fig. 2.

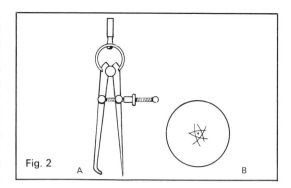

Fig. 2 A B

When boring the holes, considerable care is needed at the small glued-on piece, as it is liable to fracture. My own plan is to fix a Jennings bit in the self-centring chuck and hold the bottom end of the turning against the back centre. I then revolve the wood by hand, easing the wood forwards by turning the back centre. Once the cutters have scribed a circle I substitute a Forstner bit and bore in the same way until the hole is beyond the glued-on piece. Finally I use the Jennings bit again until the full depth has been reached. It is not advisable to use the lathe motor because the thread of the bit is liable to grab. Incidentally, the cramping up when gluing, can be done conveniently on the lathe, using the back centre to apply pressure.

When the leg is attached to the framework, clearly this method cannot be used—at any rate so far as the fixed part of the leg is concerned. Fig. 3 shows such a leg which has broken off at the narrow member. In this case I cut off the leg at the nearest member to produce two flat surfaces on which the bits could be centred and glued back the small broken piece. A cramp pressed it tightly back. I found the centre by the method already outlined, Fig. 2, and stabbed it with a pointed bradawl.

To ensure that the hole was bored in true alignment I made up the device shown in Fig. 4. I planed a block of wood to the same sectional size as the square of the leg and bored a hole through the centre with the bit to be used for the leg. This

Fig. 2 Finding centres. A odd leg calipers; B areas marked from periphery.

Fig. 3 Turned leg which has broken at the narrow member.

Fig. 3

boring could have been done on the lathe, but it seemed simpler to bore by eye from each end of the block. To opposite sides of the block I nailed two strips of wood of a width equal to the leg squares. Thus, by cramping the device to the leg as in Fig. 5, it was possible to bore a dead true hole. It will be realized that the side strips, being cramped dead level with the leg squares, ensured accurate boring.

The broken-off part of the leg was bored on the lathe as in Fig. 6, the precautions already men-

tioned being taken. Incidentally, the dowel should have a groove sawn along its length to allow surplus glue to escape when being knocked in. Fig. 7 shows the leg with the dowel in position.

When the breakage is near the end, the part can be glued in place, and a hole bored in from the end after the glue has set to enable a dowel to be inserted, as in Fig. 8.

Occasionally one comes across a broken turned leg, part of which is missing. When it can be

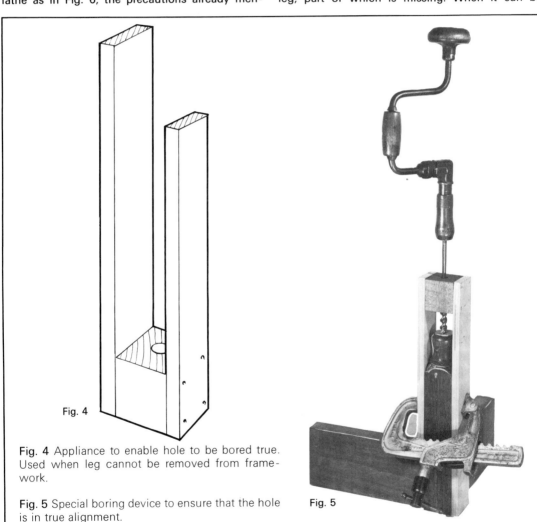

Fig. 4 Appliance to enable hole to be bored true. Used when leg cannot be removed from framework.

Fig. 5 Special boring device to ensure that the hole is in true alignment.

Fig. 4

Fig. 5

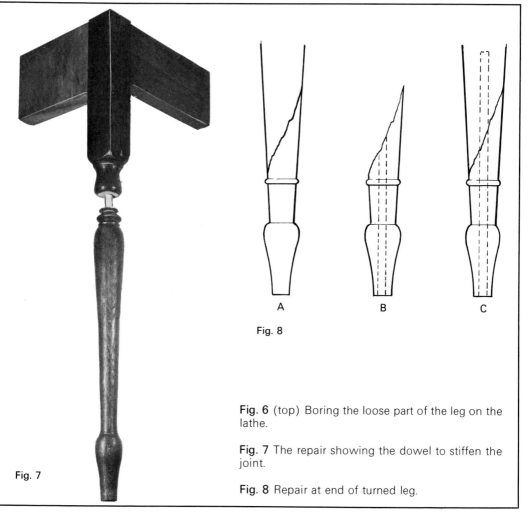

A   B   C

Fig. 8

Fig. 6 (top) Boring the loose part of the leg on the lathe.

Fig. 7 The repair showing the dowel to stiffen the joint.

Fig. 8 Repair at end of turned leg.

Fig. 7

49

Fig. 10

Fig. 12

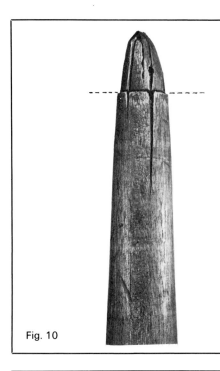

Cut off

Fig. 9

Fig. 11

Fig. 9 New part dowelled to breakage.

Fig. 10 (top left) Splintered and worn leg, castor has broken away. End is sawn off at dotted line.

Fig. 11 Shape of spigot turned to fit castor cup.

removed the simplest repair is to cut the leg off square and chuck it in the lathe, using a hollow back-centre. This enables a hole to be drilled, and the end to be turned dead square. A new replacement piece is turned with a dowel in it and glued on as in Fig. 9. When the leg can be cut back to a convenient member the new piece can be turned in its entirety, but when the smash is in a plain part it is usually more convenient to turn the new part full in size, and re-chuck the whole after gluing so that the joint can be levelled.

When the leg cannot be separated from the framework, careful boring at the end of the leg is necessary to ensure alignment. Either an assistant should be asked to stand at the side to indicate whether the brace is being held upright, or, if this is not possible, move round the leg at right angles when boring, then back again to the original position, and so on. It is easy to tell whether the brace leans to one side, but much more difficult to detect whether it leans away from or towards you.

A fairly frequent job that occurs in the repair shop is that of a table leg, the bottom of which has split in

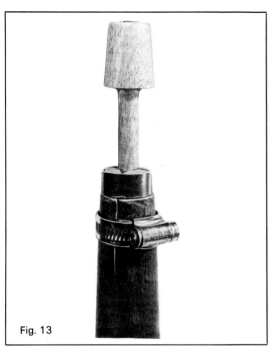

Fig. 13

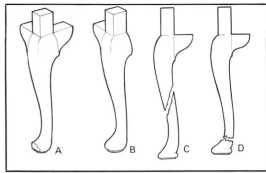

Fig. 14 Typical damage to cabriole legs. A foot chipped; B ear piece missing; C smash at short grain; D broken foot.

Fig. 12 (opp. above right) Jubilee clip tightened over broken end.

Fig. 13 (above left) Dowelled spigot fitted to leg. Note metal collar to strengthen split end.

several places, causing the castor to fall off. Quite often an attempt has been made to repair it resulting in further cracks and a multiplicity of screw holes. An example is that in Fig. 10. It would be useless to try to screw on the castor socket owing to the worn end of the wood and the many splits and holes. A new spigot in hardwood with dowel is needed, and this has to be specially turned to fit the castor socket. The dowel at one end is turned to fit into a hole to be bored in the leg, and it has therefore to be of a diameter to suit the standard size of twist bit to be used—9mm. ($\frac{3}{8}$in.), 12mm. ($\frac{7}{16}$in.), 12·5mm. ($\frac{1}{2}$in.), etc.—according to the size of the leg. Note that the shoulder is turned to a curve where it meets the dowel, Fig. 11. This is stronger than a square corner, and is on the same principle as the axle of a railway carriage wheel. The worn end of the leg has to be sawn off square to take the new spigot as shown by the dotted lines in Fig. 10.

The problem now is how to bore the hole which is truly central to receive the spigot dowel. Generally the wood is badly cracked and there may be a rough central hole, the result of a bungled repair in the past. In such a case I invariably glue in a temporary plug about 12·5mm. ($\frac{1}{2}$in.) long. It may be necessary to enlarge the existing hole. The sole purpose of the plug is to enable the bit to be started accurately in the centre. When the glue has set a pair of dividers can be used to find the centre by marking arcs in various positions around the periphery (see Fig. 2). To avoid risk of further splits when boring, a Jubilee clip should be fitted over the leg as in Fig. 12.

The existing splits in the leg are a source of weakness, of course, and where feasible a brass collar cut from suitable tubing is slipped over the end. It is necessary to cut a shallow rebate all round to take the collar. This is shown in Fig. 13 where the dowelled spigot is also visible.

When all is ready, glue is worked into the cracks and the dowel of the spigot glued and pressed home. It may be necessary to put on the collar beforehand. Finally, the screw of the Jubilee clip is tightened, so squeezing the whole firmly together. The brass ring is painted to match the wood.

Cabriole legs. These are sometimes awkward to deal with . There is often quite a lot of short grain in them which is liable to fracture. Typical breakages are shown in Fig. 14. That at A requires the wood to be cut back true and a new piece glued on as in

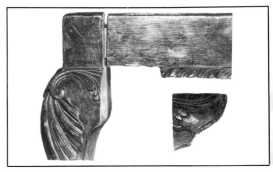

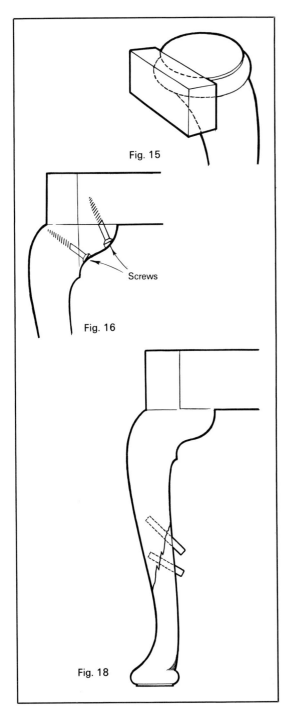

Fig. 15

Fig. 16

Screws

Fig. 18

Fig. 15 Block glued to foot. (See **Fig. 14A**.)

Fig. 16 Ear piece glued on and screwed.

Fig. 17 (above right) Ear piece to be replaced. The main joint must be made firm first.

Fig. 18 Dowel repair of broken leg. (See also Fig. 14C.)

Fig. 15. Since these club foot legs were invariably turned at the bottom, the line to which the wood has to be trimmed can be marked with dividers. It is then cut back with chisel and gouge, and where necessary with the file. Scraping and glass-papering complete the repair.

At Fig. 14B only an ear piece is missing. Usually it is more convenient to glue on a square block, and to level it after the glue has set. The shape can then be cut to match the others. It is, of course, neces-sary to level the leg to enable a good joint to be made. If the ear piece has been missing for some time it may be essential to plane the leg back to take out any rounding of the edges. Screws to supplement the glue may be advisable (see Fig. 16). In Fig. 17 the old earpiece is available, and requires only the dried glue to be scraped off. Note, however, that the main joint itself must be re-glued first if it is loose, otherwise movement of the chair in use will break off the earpiece afresh. In Fig. 17 the joint is obviously loose, but this may not be so clearly the case in other chairs. Always test the joint for movement before gluing on the earpiece.

A leg which has fractured, as at Fig. 14C, is invariably the result of badly chosen grain. The latter should run straight down, but if cut from a piece with sloping grain there is inevitably a weakness. It is doubtful whether a really lasting repair can ever be made when the chair is required for further active service, and a new leg may be needed. If, however, the breakage is fresh it can sometimes be re-glued straight away and stiffened with dowels driven in, as in Fig. 18. Sometimes screws are more satisfactory, these being recessed and the holes pelleted.

Another way which I have found more generally satisfactory is the method shown in Fig. 19 and 20. This particular leg was of ash which is a long-grained, tough timber so that the break did not run straight across the grain as it would be liable to do in the case of walnut, oak or mahogany, but was spread over a considerable length. However, the treatment would be much the same for any wood. The broken-off piece was glued back in true alignment and left to harden. At the back I cut a groove about 6mm. ($\frac{5}{16}$in.) wide by 75mm.–102mm. (3in.–4in.) long and extending about halfway or a bit more into the thickness. The bottom of this I made as flat as possible. Into this I fitted a piece of hardwood, allowing it to project so that it could be levelled later. When glued in, it made quite a strong repair. This method could be used for the break in Fig. 18.

The damage shown at Fig. 14D does not normally occur in sound wood, but does occasionally happen in walnut chairs which are susceptible to attack from the furniture beetle. Quite often the entire leg may be little more than a shell, the whole of the interior being riddled with worm tunnels. In the case of a light cabinet which is not moved about and has only to sustain the weight of the cabinet itself the replacement of the foot might be success-ful, but for a chair in everyday use the repair would be difficult. It might be possible to glue the leg in position and bore a hole to take a dowel right through from beneath. Only a small bit, say 6mm. ($\frac{1}{4}$in.) should be used as the ankle is no doubt narrow already, and in any case the strain of using a larger bit might cause further breakage. It is advisable to have an assistant to indicate whether the bit is in alignment as it may otherwise emerge at the side. The dowel should be taken well beyond the breakage so that it has ample bearing. It is advisable to use resin glue, and to endeavour to make it penetrate into the rotten wood all round the hole by working a rod up and down the latter.

Fig. 19   Fig. 20

Fig. 19 Cabriole leg fractured at the ankle.

Fig. 20 Block recessed into the back of the cabriole leg.

It is obvious, however, that such a repair by itself would not be successful on an item liable to any strain. The worm-eaten wood itself would need treatment. One way is to soak the leg in glue size for several hours so that it absorbs the size. It helps if the size is warmed. When the worm holes emerge at the outside they may enable sufficient absorption to take place, but the size must penetrate well beyond the actual breakage. Afterwards the whole thing must dry out completely before any boring takes place. Sometimes thinned-out resin glue can be used for the same purpose. It is questionable whether a badly worm-eaten chair leg would ever stand up to active service.

Tripod legs. Whilst on the subject of cabriole legs we may mention the tripod type. They are frequently in trouble owing to the strong side leverage that occurs, especially in a heavy table on which there may be considerable downward

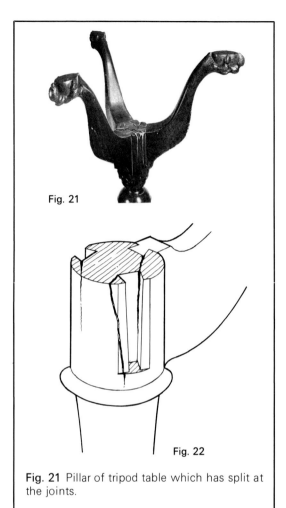

Fig. 21

Fig. 22

Fig. 21 Pillar of tripod table which has split at the joints.

Fig. 22 Smashed joints of tripod table.

pressure. In the best work the legs are slot-dovetailed in, but this involves a weakness in that the wood of the main pillar is liable to split at each side of the dovetail, as in Fig. 21. Fig. 22 shows two of the legs removed. In later work the legs were often merely dowelled, but here a different sort of weakness is inherent, the dowels being liable to pull out.

All told, the dovetail is the most satisfactory, but in any item which has to support a heavy load it is advisable to fit a specially-made metal plate, Fig.

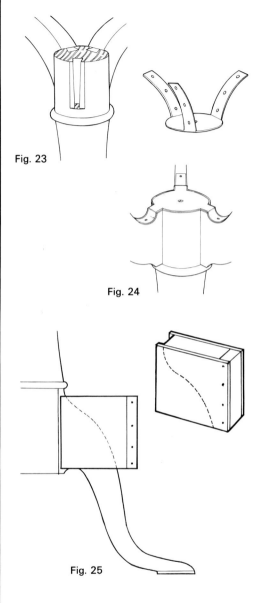

Fig. 23

Fig. 24

Fig. 25

Fig. 23 Plate for alternative shape.

Fig. 24 Strengthening plate for tripod legs.

Fig. 25 Cramping device for tripod legs.

54

23. Where practicable this should be continued a fair way along the underside of the leg, if necessary being recessed into the wood. Many old dining tables were in fact fitted with such a plate when new.

When a tripod table comes in for repair it is invariably necessary to fit a plate, because once the wood has split away there is always a weakness which will cause another collapse. One such plate is shown in Fig. 23, and it will be seen that it is bent to the shape of the leg and is screwed on. The simplest way is to cut a template of the shape in thin card, offering this up to the job and bending where necessary. This is opened flat, stuck to a piece of metal plate, and the latter fretted out and drilled for screw holes. A plate to fit a different type of leg is shown in Fig. 24.

One of the difficulties of gluing tripod legs is that of cramping. Invariably the shape is awkward so that a cramp cannot be directly applied. Sometimes a specially-made cramping block can be made, as in Fig. 25, this consisting of a centre core which clears the knee of the leg, with plywood sides which pass over the sides. A piece of rubber is placed over the work so that the polish is not injured, and the cramp applied in the most convenient position, Fig. 26. The rubber helps to prevent the block from slipping. If the latter should occur, however, it can be avoided by omitting the shaped core and putting a cramp over the plywood sides so that they grip the leg.

There are occasions when ordinary cramping is impossible and then the method in Fig. 27 will have to be followed. The leg is held in the bench vice and the pillar passed into position. A softening block is placed above and two stout laths bent and placed between this and the ceiling. These will exert sufficient pressure, though if the pillar is long, as in a standard lamp, it may be necessary to support the free end on a block or wedge-shaped piece.

The breakage in a leg of different type is shown in Fig. 28. There is short grain and this sometimes

Fig. 26 (above) How a tripod leg can be cramped.

Fig. 27 (below) Alternative cramping for tripod legs. Pillar is forced up to leg by strong laths strained between pillar and ceiling.

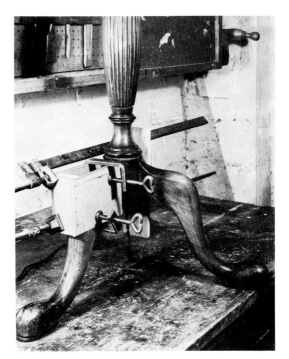

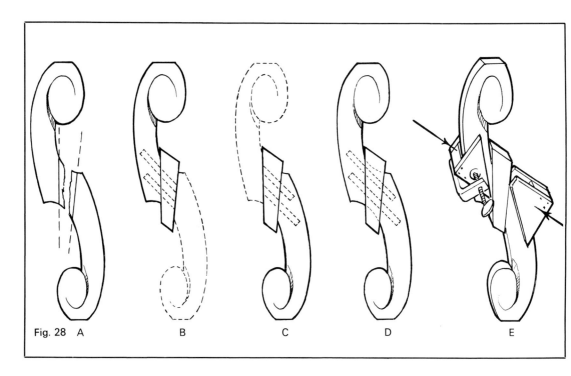

Fig. 28 A   B   C   D   E

Fig. 28 Repair to double-scrolled leg.

snaps. Strengthening dowels are needed, and the problem is how to align them. Draw the correct shape on a board either from one of the other corresponding legs, or by placing the broken pieces in correct relationship to each other and drawing around the outline. Cut back two straight surfaces so that a new block can be inserted. It is an advantage to make this slightly tapered as it has merely to be pressed farther in to make a close fit, A. Glue the block to one part of the leg only, using thin glue and interposing newspaper. Two holes can now be bored right through the block into the leg as at B. With a thin chisel lever away the block and glue it permanently to the other part of the leg.

When the glue has set the holes can be bored into the latter, the holes in the block giving correct direction to the bit. Having removed the old paper and glue from the other side the whole can be glued up with dowels, the last named having saw cuts along their length to enable surplus glue to escape. Cramping the parts can be a problem, and usually it is necessary to make up special blocks as at E. These are of the same thickness as the leg and have webs of plywood glued and nailed on at each side. They are held in position with thumbscrews, and the cramps tightened as shown. Only moderate pressure should be applied otherwise the parts may tend to slide, despite the presence of dowels.

Chapter seven

Mouldings

Mouldings are liable to damage in the course of time because in their nature they usually project. Sometimes they are worked in the solid ('stuck', as it is called), in which case they usually suffer from smashed corners and local bruises. Alternatively, they may be made separately and applied, often with the result that pieces may be loose, or missing altogether.

Stuck mouldings

When a piece of furniture is fairly heavy and the corner of the top is damaged, a really strong repair is desirable, because furniture is often lifted by the corners. A useful method is that in Fig. 1, in which the new piece is held with a dowel. The surface needs to be nicely levelled to make a good joint, and the cut across the grain should be at an angle. Trim the new piece to a neat fit, allowing it full all round and, holding it in position, mark the dowel position. One way of doing this is to place the new piece in the notch tightly up against the end and mark a line across the top surface of both pieces, as at B. This is squared down on the joining edges and a cross mark made on each with a gauge. When boring the holes, that in the main top should be a trifle nearer the inner end so a close joint at the end is assured. If by chance the fit is too tight, a shaving from the sloping end will put things right. The surfaces are levelled after setting and the moulding completed as before. Generally, it is better to deal with the end grain first.

An alternative method of fixing the dowel position is to place a pin on the notch, bring the new piece into position, and thump it so that an indentation is made on both surfaces. The two holes are bored in the pinhead position, C.

A variation of this latter method is to slant the end cut in plan as at D. The advantage is that if, after boring the holes and trying, it is found that the sloping joint is not quite tight, it is easily corrected by taking a shaving from the long edge.

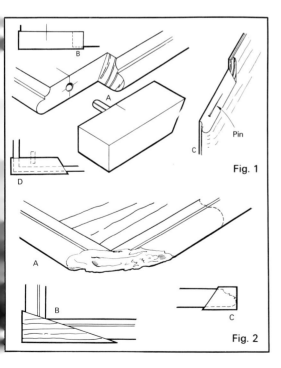

Fig. 1

Fig. 2

Fig. 1 Strong method of repairing broken corner. A dowelled repair block; B marking with square and gauge; C pin head marking; D alternative repair.

Fig. 2 Smashed corner and how it is made good.

In the case of a light table, the simpler repair in Fig. 2 can be used. The top at A has been badly smashed at the corner, and the repair is shown at B. The wood is planed back to a true surface and a new piece is cut to a generous fit and glued on. Note that the grain of the new piece must be in line with the old and as close a match as possible. To increase the gluing area the joint can be undercut, C, and the edge of the new piece made to agree. Assuming Scotch glue to be used, the wood should be heated and the glue applied to both. The piece is immediately rubbed in position and left to set.

With a small piece there is no difficulty, but if there is a tendency for it to drop off it can be held with springs made from old upholstery springs. Generally, however, Scotch glue is tacky enough to make this unnecessary. When the glue has set the new piece is levelled, care being taken not to remove the surrounding polish more than is essential to obtain a level surface. The moulding itself is formed with a small, round plane at the hollow member, and bullnose and block planes at the round member and the quirks. Glasspaper wrapped around specially-shaped blocks is used to finish off.

When the damaged corner is at the back, the simple repair in Fig. 3A is effective. For a deep bruise in the middle of a length of moulding the best way is to cut back flat to the nearest square or quirk. This does not necessarily mean the entire width of moulding. The ends are undercut in both plan and elevation as in Fig. 3B, the new piece being shaped accordingly. The advantage of this is that the ends are bound to be tight when the new piece is tapped down. All trimming and moulding to shape is done after the glue has set.

Applied mouldings

The rule about replacing broken parts as soon as possible after breakage is particularly important in the case of mouldings. For one thing, the broken piece is easily mislaid and lost, and in any case the clean broken surfaces are liable to be dubbed over so that a close joint becomes impossible. Lastly, the surfaces are soon covered with a film of grease which prevents the glue from adhering well.

Sometimes there is just local damage to a length of

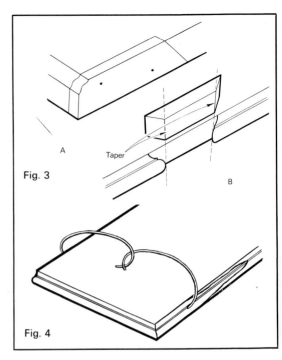

Fig. 3

Fig. 4

Fig. 3 A back corner repair; B repair in middle of moulding.

Fig. 4 Cramping with upholstery springs.

moulding, and then it can be regarded as having been worked in the solid, and a repair effected in the way already described. Generally, however, the moulding is loose and needs to be refixed, or has to be replaced.

An essential preliminary to refixing is to clean off all old, dried-up glue. On flat surfaces this can generally be done with an old chisel or similar tool. Irregular surfaces, however, need a stiff brush and hot water, especially when the repair is a second one, the first having been unskilfully done with old, thick glue.

When a length of moulding has come adrift the replacement is mostly fairly simple. Some form of cramping is usually needed, especially if the wood has sprung out of shape, and generally the most satisfactory way is to use old upholstery springs. These are cut up and bent in the form of a 'C'. One

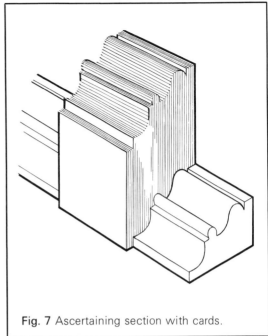

Fig. 7 Ascertaining section with cards.

Fig. 5 (above left) Repair patch held in position with pressure-sensitive tape whilst glue sets.

Fig. 6 (below left) Use of specially-shaped softening blocks when cramping a moulding.

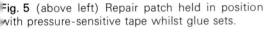

end is placed on the loose moulding and the other across the job to the nearest convenient point (see Fig. 4). Sometimes it is necessary to loop two or more together to get the required span.

Another way of holding the repair piece in place whilst the glue sets is to use pressure-sensitive tape as in Fig. 5. No moisture is used with this. The tape is pressed in position and grips immediately. When the glue has set the tape is peeled off. Sometimes cramping is essential however, especially when the moulding is heavy. In this case softening blocks under the cramp shoes are necessary, and these have to be shaped to an approximate reverse of the moulding as in Fig. 6. It is convenient to use the pressure-sensitive tape to hold the moulding in position whilst the cramps are being adjusted into position. This is shown in the illustration. Note that the softening block need not be an exact reverse of

the moulding section, so long as it enables the cramp to apply pressure where it is needed.

Mouldings which have splintered can be fixed as in Fig. 4 and 5 when the break is clean. If, however, the edges are damaged it is difficult to make a really neat job, and it is a case of choosing between the use of stopping to fill up the inevitable cracks or replacing with a new piece of moulding.

Replacement mouldings

The latter brings us to the question of making a new length of moulding. It has to be of the same section as the old, and it may be necessary to make a template to which it can be worked. Sometimes there may be an oddment with a square end which can be used, but if not a template can be made by dropping the edges of a pack of cards over the contour. If possible the cards should have square corners (not rounded as in playing cards) as it is then simple to transfer the shape by laying the sides on a piece of card and marking round with a pencil. Fig. 7 shows the idea. There is also the

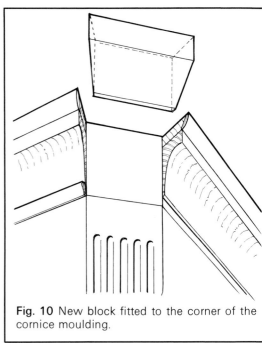

Fig. 10 New block fitted to the corner of the cornice moulding.

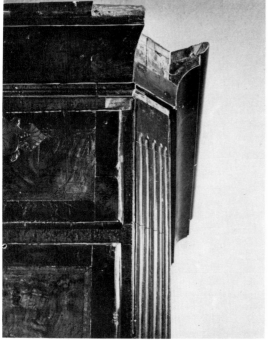

Fig. 8 (above left) Tallboy chest with typical smashed and missing mouldings. Photograph courtesy of Collins Antiques, Wheathampstead.

Fig. 9 (below left) Close-up view of the smashed corner of the chest in Fig. 8.

special Maco template which will reproduce the shape both positive and in reverse.

For small mouldings it is seldom necessary to go to the bother of a template, because ordinary measurement is all that is needed. Furthermore, if the new moulding has to be worked with the scratchstock the cutter can easily be filed to a reverse of the shape and offered to the moulding until it fits exactly. Much the same applies when the new moulding is to be worked on the French spindle, but in the case of the square-cutter block a development has to be made from the true shape, hence the necessity of drawing the latter.

A tallboy chest of drawers with the corner of the cornice missing is shown in Fig. 8. It is given enlarged in Fig. 9. In making the replacement piece

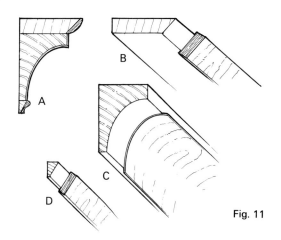

A

B

C

D

Fig. 11

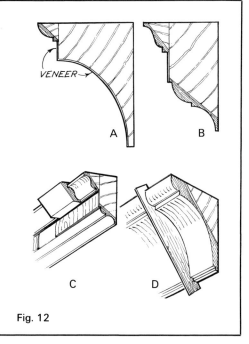

VENEER→

A

B

C

D

Fig. 12

Fig. 11 How the individual parts of the replacement moulding are built-up.

Fig. 12 Further examples of cross-grained mouldings. A and B show typical sections; C and D methods of repair.

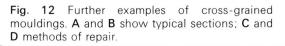

he same construction as the original could be ollowed. First a block in which the main hollow member can be worked is fitted as in Fig. 10. Then mitres are cut, care being taken to see that the block beds down at the back. At the top it finishes at the square member immediately above the hollow, and at the bottom above the small ogee mould. It is roughly chamfered at the front, and when in position a pencil is drawn round each side thus giving the final section to which it has to be worked. This shaping should be done before fixing, because it has to be veneered. The veneer is allowed to project and is levelled in line with the mitres after the glue has set.

The top member can be a plain piece bevelled at the front. It is glued in place, and cross-grained pieces of walnut are glued to the face after the glue has set. The rounded section can be worked after it is in position. In the case of the small bottom moulding, as the entire return at the side is missing, enough new moulding for the whole can be prepared and mitred in place. Note that the cross-grained walnut facing should be as thin as possible to avoid shrinkage problems. (Details, Fig. 11).

Other cornice mouldings are given in Fig. 12. Note that the flat and the large hollow members at A are veneered. The small top member at A is glued on in short, cross-grained lengths, and is sometimes fitted in a rebate. At B the solid backing wood is bevelled to enable the cross-grained walnut to be applied. Any missing parts are made good by the application of small pieces of wood, as at C, and the shape worked after the glue has set.

In the nature of things, the shrinkage across the grain tends to make open joints, and it is only the thinness of the wood which enables it to give and avoid serious trouble. Even so, joints do open sometimes, and the method of making good is to run a saw down the opening and glue in a sliver of walnut, D. Saw-cut veneer is ideal but it is difficult to obtain nowadays, and it is usually necessary to cut veneer slips on the circular saw with a planer saw fitted, or by hand.

If the veneer of the hollow member at A has pulled away, it is generally necessary to make a small reverse block to use as a caul. Glue is worked behind the veneer and the block heated and

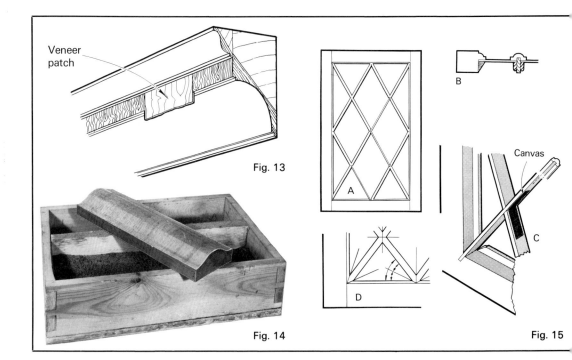

Fig. 13

B

Canvas

A

C

D

Fig. 14

Fig. 15

Fig. 13 Patch repair of veneered moulding.

Fig. 14 Ogee frieze with cross-grained veneer put down in sand tray.

Fig. 15 Barred door details. A elevation showing missing mouldings; B section of framework and moulding with bars; C how bar joints are strengthened; D angle of mitres.

cramped down with a few layers of newspaper interposed. Sometimes a sandbag made up as a roll can be used, this being heated and cramped over the moulding.

Occasionally one comes across a cornice in which the large hollow member is worked in the solid rather than veneered, as in Fig. 13. Usually the square member is veneered, however, and it is often necessary to put in a patch. This is allowed to project at the bottom and levelled afterwards.

A job that occasionally occurs is that of replacing an ogee or rounded frieze. This is a feature of Queen Anne furniture, the surface being veneered with cross-grain. A convenient way of pressing the veneer is the sand tray in Fig. 14. The whole thing is heated in an oven (when Scotch glue is being used) and two or three sheets of newspaper placed over the sand. The glued veneer is placed on the groundwork and the whole thing cramped. If the veneer tends to spring up it is advisable to press it to shape beforehand. To do this, the veneer is dampened, placed on the groundwork without glue, and cramped down in the sand tray. If the workpiece is moved back and forth it will mould the sand to the shape. When dry, it is removed, the glue applied and the original process carried out.

Barred doors

Barred doors often call for moulding replacements, though considering their fragile appearance they are surprisingly strong. If the main door framework sags it is essential that this is put right first. If possible, this should be done without taking the thing to pieces, otherwise it invariably means separating all the parts and building up again from scratch. If this is unavoidable, all the parts should

Fig. 16 Chair frame after repairs awaiting finishing and upholstery.

be numbered at the back so that they can be put back in the same places. Corresponding parts of joints should be numbered so that their positions are obvious. Unless this is done a moulding may be fixed the wrong way round.

A point to note is that the mitres always halve the overall angles of the joining mouldings. In many cases the moulding will simply have to be cut to fit against existing mitres, but when two new adjoining mouldings have to be fitted the mitres have to be cut afresh. Fig. 15D illustrates this halving of the overall angles.

Considerable strength is added to the bars or ribs if strips of fine canvas are glued in the angles, as shown at Fig. 15C, this being added after the glue in the joints has set. Some joints are halved, others finger-jointed or notched according to their positions. The bar repairs are completed first and the mouldings added afterwards. In the best work these are grooved to fit over the bars.

Chapter eight

Drawers

As in all work involving mechanical moving parts, wear is eventually inevitable. Friction takes its toll, and the strain of a drawer constantly being pulled open involves considerable wear, especially when the drawer is laden beyond its capacity, as most drawers usually are. As a rule most, if not all, of the wear can be made good, but some signs of wear cannot be wholly eradicated; neither, for that matter, is it necessary. No-one expects drawers to have sharp edges and perfect fitting after 100 or more years of active service.

At the same time the main worn or broken parts should be made good, because one fault will often start another, culminating in major repairs which could have been avoided had things been put right in time. Indeed, the rule of mending a thing as soon as possible after breakage is particularly true in drawer work. Apart from avoiding fresh troubles due to parts having to take a strain for which they were never intended, it means that the parts can be replaced whilst the edges are still sharp so that the repair is largely unnoticeable. Wear is a different matter, for it only shows itself after many years of use.

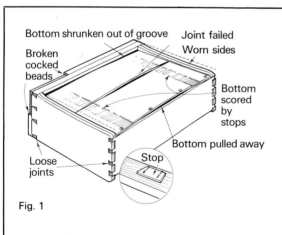

Fig. 1

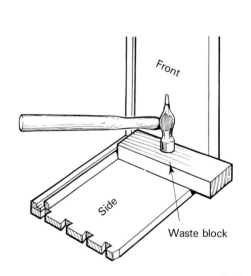

Fig. 2

Fig. 1 Worn drawer turned upside down. This shows typical faults that occur due to wear, and sometimes to overloading.

Fig. 2 Separating drawer parts.

The bureau on page 13 shows some of the typical wear and breakages that occur in drawer work; broken or loose joints, worn sides, broken and shrunken bottoms, worn runners, etc. These are mostly shown in Fig. 1. Other defects such as broken cocked beads, blemishes caused by the replacement of Victorian turned knob handles, worn or smashed lock bolts, mortises, and so on will be dealt with later; also troubles that arise in veneered work.

Loose joints. When the corner joints of a drawer are loose there is only one thing to be done about it. The parts have to be separated and re-glued. Remove the bottom by withdrawing the screws (or nails). If any joints in the bottom have failed put corresponding marks on the underside so that they can be reassembled in the same positions. Often a thump with the flat palm of one's hand will separate the sides from front and back, but if they are more obstinate a waste batten should be placed across the inside and this tapped with the hammer, Fig. 2. Without this precaution the wood may easily split owing to the local blow, and in any case the wood might be bruised.

It will be found that the joints are covered with a layer of old dried-up glue, and this should be removed. Often it will scrape off easily with a chisel, but be careful not to cut into the wood, because the probability is that the joint is a loose fit already. Sometimes damping with hot water is a help but do not flood on the water.

Assuming that the bottom edges of the sides are badly worn as in Fig. 1, it is necessary to glue on new pieces of the same kind of wood, and I invariably find it easier to do this whilst the parts are separated, Fig. 3. Plane the bottom edge to a line parallel with the groove which holds the bottom. When there is a drawer bottom slip which is not loose it can be left in position. The planing is best done on the shooting board with the grooved slip uppermost. Then when the new piece is planed on the shooting board it can be with the inside downwards, thus ensuring the two going together in alignment. This new piece can be of a width equal to the combined thickness of the side and the slip. Its thickness should allow for fitting after assembling. Incidentally, if the wear is so great that it is necessary to plane into the groove, it is essential to widen the groove in the new piece to

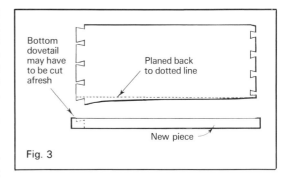

Bottom dovetail may have to be cut afresh

Planed back to dotted line

New piece

Fig. 3

Fig. 3 Making good worn lower edges of sides when drawer can be dismantled.

the original width to enable the bottom to be slid in afterwards. This can be done either by running a shallow rebate along the inner edge of the new piece, or by passing the side over the circular saw after the new piece has been glued in position. Generally it is not possible to use the hand plough because of the restricted width of the soleskate, which leaves the corners of the cutter liable to dig in.

The drawer can now be reassembled. Generally it is enough to tap in with a hammer over a waste batten, but if the parts are so loose that they are liable to drop out, cramping may be necessary. Put waste battens beneath the shoes with newspaper interposed to prevent the blocks from sticking. If the joints are really loose it is a help to rub in with the fingers a mixture of glue and fine sawdust of the same kind of wood as the sides. To do this the cramps will have to be just short of the joints. Wipe away the surplus with a slightly damp rag before the glue hardens. In all cases test for squareness. When set the drawer can be fitted.

Worn sides. If the joints are not loose it is necessary to make good the wear in another way. The majority of the wear will be towards the back, and the sides will have to be cut back to make a good joint. The plane cannot be used in the ordinary way because of the projection of the front, and the only way is to use the chisel and bullnose plane, though it is possible to use a smoothing plane towards the back. It is a help to finish off with coarse glasspaper held tightly round a flat block of wood. If the wear is short of the groove, glue on the new piece as in Fig. 4. Sometimes in really bad cases the wear is right into the groove, and it is then necessary to work a shallow rebate in the new piece so that the original width of groove is maintained. When the glue has set, the drawer can be fitted as though it were a new one. Do not use nails in fixing the new pieces, except half-driven in temporarily merely to hold the parts whilst the glue sets. Even if punched in, the wood is eventually worn away, and the nails cut deep scores in the runners. The new pieces must, of course, be slightly full in size to allow for fitting when the glue has set. In any case the new pieces are glued to the sides and drawer bottom moulding only, not to the bottom itself.

Drawer bottoms. These are invariably made up of two, and sometimes three, pieces jointed side by side to make up the width of material needed. The joints frequently fail over the years owing to the weight imposed on them or because of too much material being forced into the drawer. A second point is that, since the fixing is at the back, the front is liable to pull out of its groove as a result of shrinkage, shown clearly in Fig. 1. It is true that many drawers were made with the bottom extra wide so that it projected at the back, enabling the bottom to be pushed forward and re-fixed. But this extra allowance is not always found, or in some cases may be inadequate, and it is then necessary to join on a piece at the back.

The broken joints should be re-planed and glued afresh. As the bottoms are invariably thin it is not practicable to assemble the parts one above the other in the vice as they would be liable to topple over. They must be glued on a flat board, and a complication that often arises is that the parts will not lie flat. The front piece especially is liable to bow downwards owing to its having pulled out of its groove and having to withstand the bulk and weight of things forced in. The result is that the ends stand up as in Fig. 5, when laid down flat. The simplest plan is to put heavy weights at the ends as in Fig. 6, and glue-rub the other piece up to it. Newspaper beneath prevents the wood from sticking to the board. Some similar arrangement may be necessary when planing the joint on the shooting board.

Fig. 4 shows the drawer from beneath after finishing. The strip of canvas may not be needed,

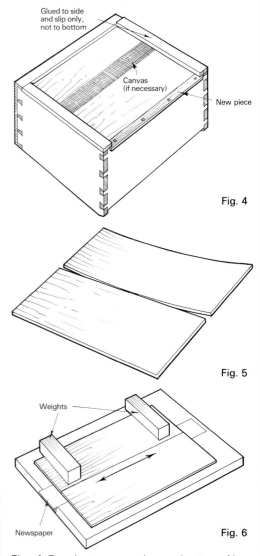

Fig. 4 Repairs to worn drawer bottom. New pieces glued to bottom edge of sides to make up wear.

Fig. 5 Failed joint in drawer bottom. One piece has become bent owing to weight.

Fig. 6 Rubbing joint of drawer bottom. The weights keep the wood flat. See **Fig. 5**.

but it is sometimes required when the bottom has been seriously weakened by being scored deeply on the underside by scraping over drawer stops (see Fig. 1) or when the bottom has a split which follows the grain rather than being a joint failure. It is also a precaution to use canvas when it is anticipated that the drawer will have to take heavy items. Sometimes to economize in the cost of repairs the canvas is applied without re-jointing, but the latter makes a better job. In modern work, of course, plywood or hardboard is used, and these materials are in many ways more satisfactory as no jointing is needed and there is no shrinkage problem.

Older drawers frequently had the grain of the bottom running from front to back, but it was not a very satisfactory arrangement because the wood had to be rigidly fixed to the sides and, since shrinkage was inevitable over so great a width, splits, usually at the joints, were bound to occur. It will be realized that when the grain runs from side to side there is no problem because, although fixed at the back, the bottom is free to shrink backwards along the side grooves and out of that in the front. That is why in the best work the bottom was made to project at the back so that, when shrinkage occurred, the bottom could be pushed forwards and re-fixed at the back. It is the old story that shrinkage does not matter except when you try to stop it.

Fig. 7 shows two ways in which the bottoms were fixed. At A the sides are rebated, the bottom put in, and slips glued on top. At B there is not even a rebate, the bottom being fixed directly to the sides and slips glued on top.

Repair involves replacement of the slips, new pieces being glued on. Occasionally the wear may be so excessive that the bottom scrapes at the back. A certain amount of levelling with the rebate plane is necessary and extra thick slips glued on. These are planed as may be required to make a fit after the glue has set. Either use nails to hold the slips whilst the glue is setting, withdrawing them afterwards, or use the old upholstery springs as cramps as at Fig. 4, page 58. The drawer in Fig. 8 has its grain running from front to back.

Cocked beads. Many old drawers of the eighteenth and nineteenth centuries and later had

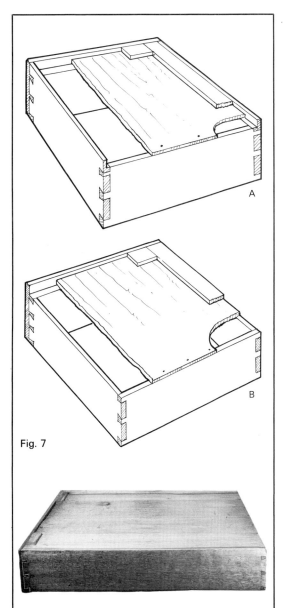

Fig. 7

Fig. 7 Older types of drawers in which grain of bottom runs from front to back.

Fig. 8 (below) Old drawer in which grain of bottom runs from front to back.

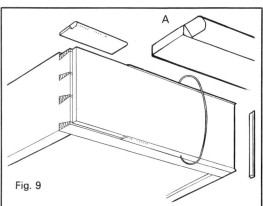

Fig. 9

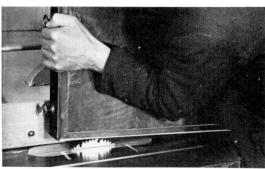

Fig. 9 Cocked bead replacement. Special half-mitre at top corners is shown at **A**.

Fig. 10 (above right) Cutting worn edge of drawer on the circular saw. Note chalk mark on table showing limit of movement. See also **Fig. 11**.

Fig. 11 (below right) Cutting other side of worn edge. See also **Fig. 10**.

cocked beads around the fronts. Their purpose, apart from having an attractive appearance, was to protect the edges of the veneer frequently used on the fronts. Some measure of their usefulness in this respect can be gained from the fact that they themselves have frequently suffered considerable damage over the years. Sometimes complete new lengths of moulding have to be fitted, though generally only odd parts have been broken off. If the broken-off part can be replaced straight away the repair can usually be neatly made, but more generally missing pieces must be replaced.

Along the bottom and sides the bead fits in a rebate, the dovetails of the sides being curtailed somewhat so that the rebate (which lines up with the lap) can be of reasonable width. This rebate may also occur along the top edge, but more generally the bead is made to cover the full thickness of the front, and this makes a slight complication at the mitres as shown in Fig. 9. Whereas the bottom corners are plain, those at the top have to be mitred at the front only, A.

All cocked beads should be worked to the finished

width so that they need only rubbing with glass-paper held around a shaped block to make them level with adjoining beads. They are glued in position, and the simplest way of holding them whilst the glue sets is to use old upholstery springs as in Fig. 9. When the end beads are fixed two or more springs can be linked together. Frequently veneer pins are driven in, but it is better to avoid their use.

When a circular saw is available this can be used to make the worn bottom edge level. The fence is set so that the saw is in the correct position to make the cut when the top edge of the drawer side is held against it. Each side requires a slightly different treatment. In the one case the back of the drawer can be pushed forwards as in Fig. 10 and the cut stopped when it is just short of the front. This cannot be done at the other side, and it is necessary to drop on to the saw as Fig. 11 shows. To make sure that the cut is started in the right position, a chalk mark is made on the saw table as shown, this being the position where the drawer front is held. At the end of the cut the drawer can be pushed right through, of course. In both cases the cut

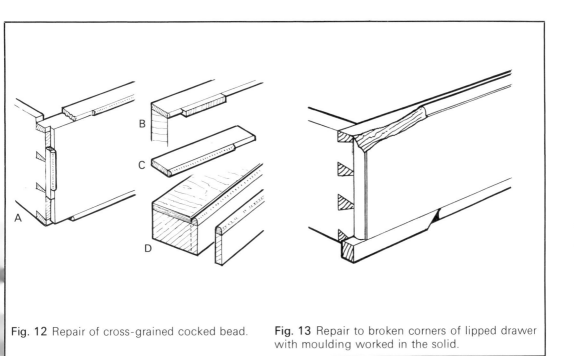

Fig. 12 Repair of cross-grained cocked bead.

Fig. 13 Repair to broken corners of lipped drawer with moulding worked in the solid.

immediately at the drawer front will have to be made with the hand saw. Before starting, make sure that there are no nails.

Occasionally a walnut chest turns up with cross-grained cocked beads, and the repair of these can work out quite costly as it involves making new parts mounted on strips of long-grained stuff as at Fig. 12A. It can be quite exasperating because frequently just the cross-grained wood has broken away leaving the long-grained backing intact. When only small sections are missing it is practicable to glue on pieces of cross-grained stuff as at B, these being levelled after the glue has set, the bullnose plane being specially handy for working the rounded section. This is followed by glasspaper used on a hollow rubber. When, however, the entire bead is missing it is necessary to make up new lengths. I generally find the best way to glue cross-grained walnut to a backing is as at Fig. 12D. After planing the edge straight, I work the bead with a small bead plane and slice off the entire thing as shown. After gluing to the drawer edge, the front slightly proud, I level it to the adjoining bead. It is one of those jobs for

which there is little to show for the time taken and for this reason repairs are sometimes made with lengths of straight-grained walnut. It is a question of how much a customer is prepared to spend — and sometimes whether he realizes that the original cocked bead was cross-grained!

Overlapping drawers. When the front is of solid wood there is often a moulding around the edges, this overlapping the carcase. Frequently the corners are damaged, and this entails cutting away the wood to a clean surface and fitting a fresh piece of the same kind of wood as in Fig. 13. It makes a rather stronger joint if it can be undercut. Incidentally, it is most important that the inner or rebate side is levelled correctly afterwards otherwise the new patch will strike the drawer rail every time the drawer is closed. The outer moulded section can be finished to shape afterwards with the bullnose plane and finished with glasspaper held over a wood rubber of reverse section.

A rather more complicated moulding repair occurs on some walnut period furniture in which the moulding is cross-grained and the drawer front

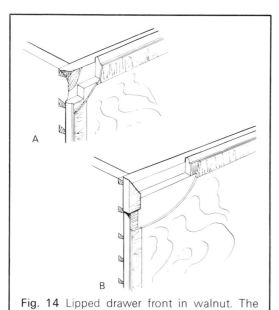

Fig. 14 Lipped drawer front in walnut. The moulding is cross-grained. Breakage invariably pulls away the face veneer.

veneered. The trouble usually is that the breaking away of the moulding brings part of the veneer away with it. These mouldings were invariably formed by gluing pieces of walnut with the grain running cross-wise into a rebate worked around the front, as shown in Fig. 14. The front was veneered, usually with cross-banded edges, and the moulding worked last.

It is first necessary to make good the moulding. Fig. 14 shows how the pieces are glued in, the corners being mitred if necessary. When the glue has set the front surface is levelled and the veneer made good. This is dealt with in the chapter on veneer repairs, page 89. To finish off, the edges are trimmed level with the adjoining mould-ing, with a sharp cutting gauge to the moulding width. A cut is made right through the veneer, and the moulding worked to shape with the bullnose plane and finished with glasspaper held over a wood rubber. The tallboy chest shown on page 60 has drawers of this type.

Removing wood knobs. A task frequently facing the repairer is that of removing wood

knobs from an eighteenth century chest. It was common practice in the Victorian period to 'modernize' old pieces in this way, the original brass handles being removed and replaced with wood knobs (see photograph on page 18). Fixing the latter entailed boring right through the drawer front and frequently the knobs were glued in. When they are loose there is no difficulty in their removal, but care has to be taken with a tight knob not to disturb the adjoining surface, especially where the latter is veneered. Where the glue is obviously gripping the veneered surface it is usually simpler to cut away the shoulder of the knob by tapping with a chisel, as in Fig. 15.

The grain of the knob always runs front to back so that the shoulder chips away easily without the chisel touching the drawer front. The knob can generally be loosened by gripping tightly and turning first one way then the other. Sometimes it is necessary to strike the dowel of the knob from inside the drawer, an oddment of dowel smaller than that of the knob being used.

The filling of the resultant hole depends upon whether the new brass handle plate covers it or not. If it does, a piece of dowel can be used — sometimes that of the old knob is suitable. How-ever, if it will show, it is necessary to turn a pellet as in Fig. 16, this having the grain running crosswise. When the grain of the front is really decorative, it may be necessary to recess it slightly and glue in a piece of veneer.

Note that the inside of the drawer front needs to be finished off neatly, and as the hole is often burred over at the edges, it is necessary to cut in new pieces. My own method (when the customer was prepared to pay for it) was to chop diamond-shaped recesses about 3mm. ($\frac{1}{8}$in.) deep and glue in corresponding new pieces of the same kind of wood as the drawer front, as shown in Fig. 17, levelling it after the glue had set.

An unskilful repair to a drawer knob is shown in Fig. 18 and 19. At some time the knob has pulled right out and, to enable it to be fixed, someone has added a wood block inside and driven a screw through it. It is a crude device in any case and is liable to fail because the screw enters end grain in the knob and would have a poor hold. In restoration the whole thing would be removed,

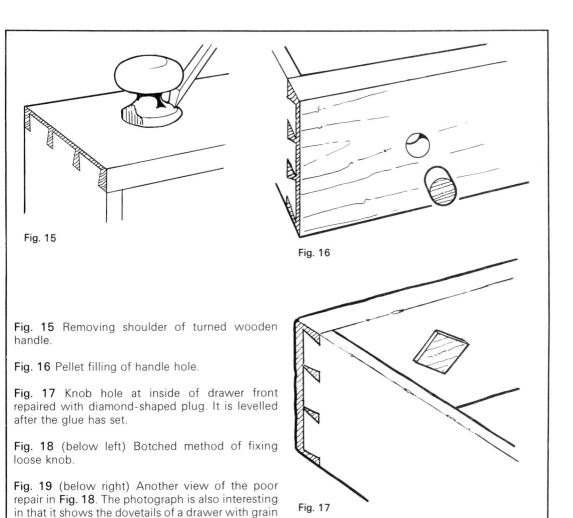

Fig. 15

Fig. 16

Fig. 15 Removing shoulder of turned wooden handle.

Fig. 16 Pellet filling of handle hole.

Fig. 17 Knob hole at inside of drawer front repaired with diamond-shaped plug. It is levelled after the glue has set.

Fig. 18 (below left) Botched method of fixing loose knob.

Fig. 19 (below right) Another view of the poor repair in Fig. 18. The photograph is also interesting in that it shows the dovetails of a drawer with grain of bottom running from front to back.

Fig. 17

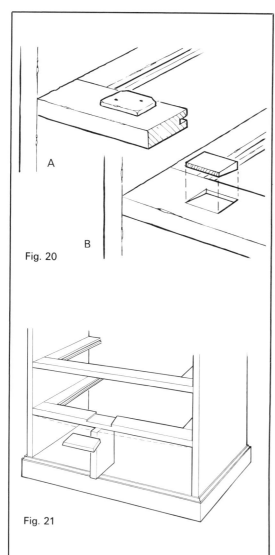

A

B

Fig. 20

Fig. 21

Fig. 20 Drawer stops. **A** usual fixing with glue and nails; **B** stronger method recessed into sloping notch.

Fig. 21 Straightening bowed drawer rail. The wood post beneath is pushed in temporarily. If it is tapered at top and bottom the extent of straightening can be adjusted.

and replaced by brass handles, the hole being made good by the method outlined above.

Drawer stops. When the drawer has had a lot of wear the stops often scrape the bottom as the drawer is moved. It is useless, therefore, to replace stops unless the drawer sides have been made good. Usually the position of the stops is obvious, but account has to be taken of any damage to the rear of the front owing to frequent closing. In some cases it is better to fix them in a fresh position. When the drawer front is flush a gauge set to the thickness of the front enables the position on the rail to be marked. Fix with glue and a top couple of pins, punching the latter below the surface. The grain of the stops should preferably run from front to back as the end grain resists wear better.

In nearly every case in old furniture drawer stops were merely glued and nailed in position as at Fig. 20A. In the case of a heavy drawer I have sometimes found it an advantage to cut a sloping recess to hold the stop as at Fig. 20B. The back of the recess resists the jolt whereas the stop at A relies purely on the glue and nails to hold it.

Drawer rails. Drawer rails, curved slightly in the centre, can give trouble. If between two drawers it affects both. Fig. 21 shows how a curved rail can be made straight permanently. It is useless, of course, forcing a wooden post between the faulty rail to raise it up, then damping in the hope that, by the time it has dried properly (in the course of a few days) it will remain straight when the supporting post is removed. It may do so, but the curve invariably returns as badly as ever.

I recommend the fitting of flat wedges of wood in the centre, the ends being a dovetail fit as in Fig. 21. If the bend is downwards, the wedge goes to the top and vice versa. Before cutting the recess for the wedge force a wooden post beneath the bearer. The post should be 3mm. ($\frac{1}{8}$in.) longer to force the bearer 3mm. ($\frac{1}{8}$in.) out of true alignment. Having cut the recess and fitted the wedge the post is knocked away. The wedge, being slightly longer than apparently necessary (as a result of the extra lift given by the post), becomes squeezed tightly in position, thereby checking the tendency of the bearer to bend downwards. Thus the bearer becomes and remains straight. The exact length of the wedge can be found by experiment. The simplest way is to make it extra wide and cut the ends to a taper, thus allowing a certain amount of adjustment. Should there still be a slight curvature, a rather longer wedge will rectify matters. After the right length of wedge has been found, it is glued in position. Some cabinet makers dislike having the wedge joint showing at the face of the bearer. They prefer to fit it inwards 12·5mm. (½in.) or so. There is no difficulty when there is an applied facing. It is removed, the wedge fitted in, and the facing then replaced. The treatment of drawer runners is dealt with in Chapter three.

When a drawer will not open. This trouble is sometimes encountered, and may be the result of casting in the wood, a faulty lock or a missing key. It is clear that the remedies adopted must do as little damage as possible. It is simple enough to insert a crowbar and give it a wrench, but the last state of the work will be worse than the first. Slight damage in some circumstances may be inevitable, but it must be kept to a minimum.

The commonest cause of not being able to open a drawer is that it has been locked and the key either fails to turn, or it has been entirely lost. Since locks are screwed on from inside the simplest plan when practicable is to undo the screws from inside.

If it is not a top drawer remove the drawer above and see if you can locate the screws, using a long screwdriver, as in Fig. 22. If there is no dustboard, this is generally possible. If this can be done, the drawer will usually pull out, leaving the lock to fall inside. Another way is to take off the back and see if you can get at it that way. Again, the drawer above will have to be withdrawn, and possibly the dustboard.

Should it be the top drawer, things are more difficult. In some cases it may be possible to remove the top, taking off the back first, but generally this cannot be done as the screw heads are invariably covered by the drawer itself. One plan (which can also be applied to other drawers if the foregoing methods fail) is to attempt to punch off the lock by placing a punch against the lock pin and striking it. The screws are generally small and will usually give. The lock, of course, is spoilt and a new one will have to be fitted. It is a help if you take off the back and ask an assistant to push

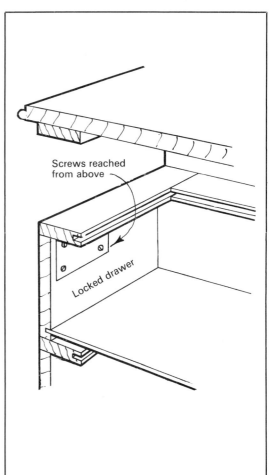

Screws reached from above

Locked drawer

Fig. 22 Section drawing showing how to tackle a locked drawer. Removing lock when key is lost.

the drawer forward from the back whilst punching.

Reverting again to lower drawers, if a dustboard prevents access from above, one plan is to cut a recess opposite the bolt from above and endeavour to punch down the bolt, as in Fig. 23. Cheap locks often succumb to this treatment. The recess will have to be plugged afterwards and a hole cut to suit the new lock. If you examine the other locks you will see the position of the bolt on the lock.

If the drawers are long, it is sometimes possible to

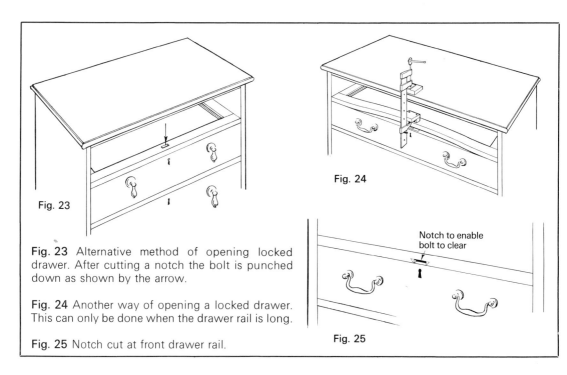

Fig. 23

Fig. 24

Notch to enable
bolt to clear

Fig. 25

Fig. 23 Alternative method of opening locked drawer. After cutting a notch the bolt is punched down as shown by the arrow.

Fig. 24 Another way of opening a locked drawer. This can only be done when the drawer rail is long.

Fig. 25 Notch cut at front drawer rail.

bend up the rail above the drawer, as shown in Fig. 24. Two pieces of wood are screwed together to form an L shape, and the whole screwed above the rail. By fixing a cramp as shown, the rail can sometimes be bent upwards sufficiently for the bolt to clear. It is a rather drastic procedure and must not be overdone or the rail may snap. Short drawers cannot be dealt with in this way.

Should all the above methods fail and a key to turn the lock be unobtainable, the only way is to cut a notch in the front of the rail opposite the bolt to enable the latter to clear, as in Fig. 25. Afterwards a neat dovetailed patch can be let in as shown by the dotted line, and a fresh recess cut to suit the new bolt.

One other method that can sometimes be adopted is to remove the back and endeavour to take out the drawer bottom. This is sometimes handy when it is the top drawer which is at fault, and it is impossible to remove the top. The bottom invariably fits in grooves in the front and sides and

is nailed or screwed to the back. Undo the screws or prise down the bottom and try to slide out the latter. You can then probably get at the screws holding the lock.

If the lock is not the cause of the trouble, it is due either to the wood having swollen or to something in the drawer catching against the rail above. In the former case remove the back and, holding a piece of wood against the back, first at one side, then the other, tap with a hammer. This will generally free the drawer. If the back is a fixture, remove the other drawers if possible and endeavour to lever the drawer out at the back. Alternatively, if the whole piece is placed in a dry atmosphere for a while it will generally shrink the timber, enabling the drawer to be pulled out. In any case, furniture which is damp should be allowed to dry out thoroughly.

Should something be catching inside, insert the blade of a thin knife (such as a table knife) along the top edge. This will generally move the obstruction and enable it to clear.

Chapter nine

Doors

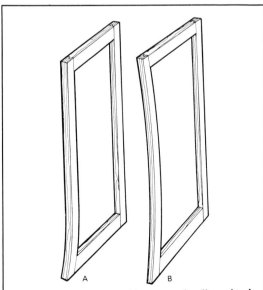

Fig. 1 Door frame with warped stiles. At **A** the warping is purely local; in **B** the warping is over the whole length.

A common fault found in doors is that of loose joints in the framework. For a satisfactory repair, the only way is to dismantle the whole, make good any damage, and re-glue. Quite often the trouble is due to the mortises having split, and these will have to be put right. In old pieces any such splits may be half-filled with dirt and old furniture cream, and this will have to be cleaned out as far as possible because glue will not grip over it. Sometimes the broken blade of an old hacksaw can be inserted, and used to clean the surface as far as is possible, but in any case it is usually possible to force open the split without further breaking to facilitate the cleaning.

Dismantling. However, the first problem is that of dismantling the whole. When all the joints are loose it is easy, but there may still be some tight ones. Examine first to see whether there are any nails or wood pegs holding the parts together. If not, it may be that a racking movement made simultaneously with outward pulling may help, but be careful not to carry this to excess, as it may break the tenon. Sometimes a block of wood held against the edges of the stile and struck with the hammer may do the trick. In bad doors, when there is no veneer to worry about, the parts can be warmed (preferably from the back) as this softens animal glue. In some cases it may be possible to deal with the faulty joints without touching those which hold. It is helpful to cut round joints with a knife before separating as it avoids splintering out adjoining wood.

All old dried-up glue must be got rid of. Sometimes it is easier to scrape it off; in other cases a warm, damp swab will enable it to be removed, but avoid flooding on water.

In subsequent fitting, if the mortise has been split open and glued up, it is advisable to put a thumb-screw with a block of wood beneath the shoe to prevent the chance of its being split open afresh. If the tenon is a really loose fit it may be necessary to add a slip of veneer to each side. This is then eased down with a file to a good fit, care being taken to see that the parts are flush at the sides when offered together.

Winding. This is an annoying fault, and one which is often difficult to correct. Generally it is due to the wood of the framework having twisted in its length, but occasionally one comes across cases in which it is due to the door having been re-glued at some period and not tested for freedom from winding. In the former case look along the length of each member, and it will invariably be found that one has become bent in its length and, unless this can be put right, there is little that can be done. In Fig. 1A the stile has become bent at its lower end, the curve being local, and it is obvious that the corner will either stand out or bend in. At B the whole length of the stile is bent. When the corner bends inwards, a possible cure is to cramp the door face downwards to the bench so that the stile is straightened and make one or two saw cuts across it as in Fig. 2B. Wedge-shaped pieces of hardwood are tapped into the kerfs and the cramps released to see whether the stile remains straight. It may be necessary by trial and error to tap in the wedges more to ensure straightness. When satisfactory the wedges are removed and glued, and a final test made. The projecting wedges are levelled after the glue has set.

A more generally satisfactory plan, however, is to make tapered notches as at Fig. 3A and let in corresponding blocks of hardwood. Note that the taper is across the grain so that the degree of tightening can be increased by tapping the block in further as at B. The sides of the notch are slightly undercut so that there is no tendency for the block to lift as it is knocked in. When the curve is longer, the length of the notch can be increased as in Fig. 4. Before gluing, the door should be tested to see whether the repair has had the desired effect. Generally, thumbscrews with softening blocks beneath the shoes are necessary over a long inserted block. In all cases it is invariably desirable to cramp the door down on to a flat board before inserting the block.

When the corner of the door stands out, it is more difficult to deal with, because cuts across the face of the framework are undesirable unless it can be veneered afterwards. In any case, it should be realized that the method causes kinks in the stile where the wedges occur. It is better to make several cuts fairly close together rather than just one or two. It may be that a new stile is the only answer. Sometimes an attempt is made to cramp the stile into the reverse direction and leave for as long as possible. It is doubtful whether this is successful, however, for although it may be straight

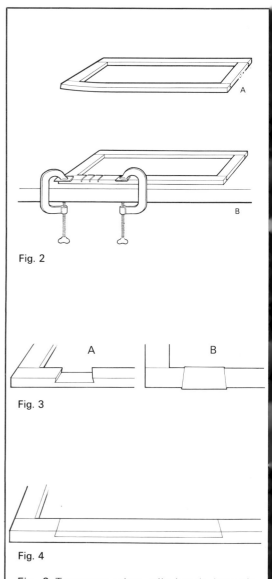

Fig. 2

Fig. 3

Fig. 4

Fig. 2 Treatment when stile bends inwards. A door on bench. Corner is forced downwards; B sawcuts across back of stile.

Fig. 3 Wedge-shaped block inserted at door back.

Fig. 4 Similar to **Fig. 3** but with longer block.

when the cramps are first released, it usually reverts to its old curvature.

In the case of a valuable antique it may be undesirable to fit a new stile, and when the framework can be dismantled the method in Fig. 5 can be followed. A cut is made at each side of the mortise right through the width of the wood up to well beyond the curve. The cuts should preferably be made on the bandsaw. Slips of wood of a thickness equal to the saw kerfs are glued in and the stile cramped straight. When set, it should hold its straightness. Note that a single cut right through the mortises is usually of no use because the slip would have to be cut through when the mortise is re-chopped. Naturally the position of the saw kerfs has to be arranged in accordance with any moulding at the edge.

Panels. Sometimes the panel of a framed door splits, and the repair is simple when it is beaded in, as it can be removed. When, however, it is grooved in, it cannot be taken from the framework, and the repair has to be made as it is.

When it is the failure of a joint, examine first to see whether the panel has been fixed in any way to the frame—glue, nails, etc. This is the likeliest cause of trouble, since the panel should be free to move in its grooves. Generally it becomes obvious if the panel is gripped between the hands at each side and an endeavour made to shift it. If it will not budge, find out what is holding it. Possibly nails driven through a moulding may be fixing it to the framework, or maybe glue has spread from the joints.

As far as is possible the old glue in the open joint should be removed, though this is difficult. Sometimes an old hacksaw blade can be inserted and worked along the joint. If it is fairly wide, a piece of cloth can sometimes be passed through and worked up and down, hot water being applied at the sides. If this is done, it is essential to leave it to dry out thoroughly before re-gluing is attempted.

Cramping a panel. To enable the parts to be brought closely together, some form of cramping is desirable. Generally the best way is to do this from the back, a pair of blocks being glued each side of the crack, enabling a cramp to be applied. A long panel generally needs two pairs of blocks. In the

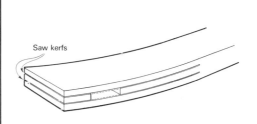

Saw kerfs

Fig. 5

Fig. 6

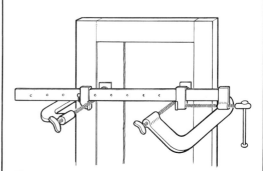

Fig. 7

Fig. 5 Alternative method of correcting warping. This is possible only when the framework can be dismantled.

Fig. 6 Blocks glued to back of panel to enable cramp to be applied.

Fig. 7 Another method of cramping panel. This is used when screws cannot be inserted in the back.

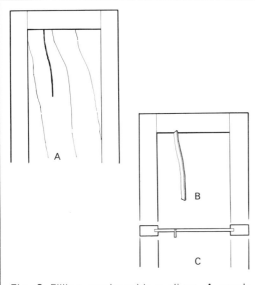

Fig. 8 Filling cracks with a sliver. **A** crack opened at thin end with saw; **B** sliver inserted; **C** section showing sliver.

case of a polished surface, however, it is useless to glue the blocks, because glue will not hold over polish. It may be possible to use small screws to fix the blocks, the holes being filled in after the removal of the blocks. If this is not practicable, a more satisfactory way is to fix G cramps on the panel, these bridging over the framework, and apply a sash cramp over these as in Fig. 7. Glue is worked into the open joint with a slip of veneer and the cramp tightened, care being taken to see that the two parts of the panel go together flush. Use the simple device shown at Fig. 23C, page 26.

When a panel has developed a natural shake which tapers in its length, it is useless to attempt to cramp it together, because it is under stress and would eventually open again. In this case it is better to fill it in with a sliver which approximates to the shape, as in Fig. 8. Often it is necessary to open the crack slightly at the narrow end, using a fine saw. In any case, the dirt should be cleaned out as far as possible with a broken hacksaw blade.

The sliver should be slightly tapered in section so that it makes a close fit at the front. Here again,

make sure that the two parts are level when the sliver is put in. Otherwise there will be complications when the surface is levelled.

Flush doors. Flush doors can present an extremely difficult problem, and in some cases there may be no satisfactory repair. They are made in various ways, but in really old pieces there are two main methods of construction. Quite small doors are sometimes simply single pieces of wood, but this is seldom the case in a door of any size, because for a door to be reliable it has to be straight-grained, and this is not specially interesting to look at. Consequently, such doors are veneered, and the groundwork is sometimes made up of narrow strips glued together side by side.

Likely faults, apart from the veneer, are that the groundwork has warped. To correct this without stripping off the veneer is difficult. Methods of lifting veneer are outlined on page 93. It is invariably necessary to flat the veneer once raised, and when there is a built-up pattern it is essential that the parts are marked so that they can be re-assembled in the correct places. Generally, the safest plan is to lay out the parts on a flat board and stick pieces of gummed tape to hold the parts together. This is specially desirable when the veneer has broken up into small pieces.

A flush door with clamped construction is given in Fig. 9. This is shown in some exaggeration to make clear the result of shrinkage. The main panel has pulled in along the clamps, and a split has developed. Such faults are difficult to correct, and when the movement is only slight it is frequently advisable to accept it because the cure might be as bad as the fault. However, the trouble can sometimes be put right by the method given for a flush panel on page 92, where an unsightly crack running right across the face is dealt with. A form of construction liable to similar faults is the framed door with flush panel in Fig. 10. The usual trouble is that the panel shrinks, causing stress marks in line with the joints between panel and framework. The cure could be costly in that the entire veneer might have to be stripped off and pieced together with clean joints, but it would be difficult to eradicate the stress marks. In any case, the groundwork would have to be made good first. In a really bad case a new groundwork might be needed. When the grain of the veneer is quite plain it

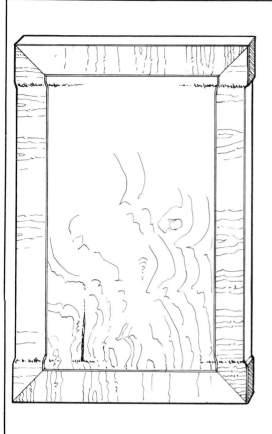

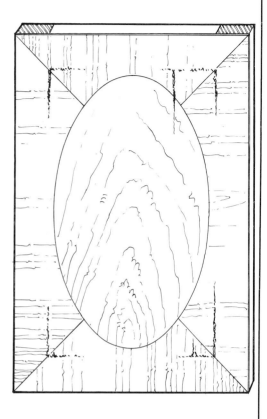

Fig. 9 Flush door with clamped construction. Note stress marks and cracks due to shrinkage.

Fig. 10 Framed door with flush panel. Note stress marks on the veneer.

might be possible to glue in a sliver along a straight crack, but to attempt to do so on a richly-figured veneer would be useless. It would simply shriek out.

Tambour doors. The usual trouble with these is the perishing of the canvas back so that it tears at the joints. Sometimes parts are missing and these have to be replaced. At the outset a trial should be made to see whether the length is sufficient. All old canvas must be removed, and usually the easiest method is to use a swab dampened with hot water.

It is as well to number the parts and replace them in the same order. For the assembling, a special tray is prepared, as shown in Fig. 11, the two edgings keeping the ends level. The end strip against which the pieces are pressed must be exactly square, as otherwise there will be difficulty in fitting. The parts are lightly cramped together, a batten being placed over the whole to prevent their springing up.

Scotch glue is used to fix the new canvas. If, as often happens in an old piece, there are gaps at the edges of the pieces, the edges should be rubbed

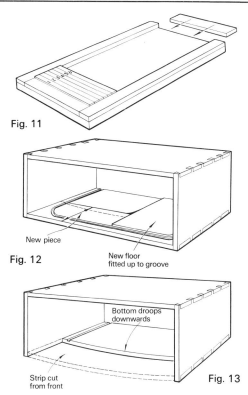

Fig. 11

New piece

Fig. 12   New floor
fitted up to groove

Bottom droops
downwards

Strip cut
from front   **Fig. 13**

Fig. 11 Framework for assembling a tambour. The old members are numbered for easy replacement.

Fig. 12 Tambour box with warped bottom.

Fig. 13 Repair to tambour box in **Fig. 12**.

with candlegrease to prevent any glue which may exude from sticking the whole together.

Various methods are adopted to enable the tambour to be fed in. Sometimes there is a temporary groove which leads straight out at the back, this being filled in after the tambour has been fed in. In this case the filling must be removed and replaced after feeding in the tambour. An examination will reveal this, but in any case it is usually necessary to remove the back.

Sometimes the tambour jams or drops out owing to the top or bottom having warped. This is often troublesome to deal with. It may be possible to insert a centre upright which will bring the two parts parallel, but the effect should be tried out first before actually fitting it.

It may be that the running is still too bad, calling for other remedies. I recall a repair I once made to the tambour box of a bow-front sideboard. The bottom had badly bowed downwards so that the tambour dropped out. I cut off a strip about 50mm. (2in.) wide from the front as in Fig. 12 and replaced it with a new, straight strip in which the groove was worked. The difference in level at the middle I ignored. After gluing it in position I cut the curved grooves at the corners to align with the existing ones. There was necessarily a marked difference at the middle, but I covered the whole thing with a sheet of 3mm. ($\frac{1}{8}$in.) plywood, fitting this just short of the groove as in Fig. 13. Is it justifiable to use plywood on an old piece? Your guess is as good as mine. Personally I am not sure, but it certainly did the trick, and when the edges were painted it was difficult to detect. Perhaps a completely new bottom would have been better?

Chapter ten

Faults in Table and Similar Tops

The chief troubles that arise with table and similar tops are those of warping, broken joints and splits. Blemishes in veneer are dealt with in Chapter eleven, but it is worth noting that it may be possible to remove the veneer and cut the groundwork into strips about 50mm.–75mm. (2in.–3in.) wide. These are shot into clean joints to make a flat top and glued together. This involves gluing on an extra strip as in Fig. 1 to make up the loss of width in sawing and planing. The glued surface of the veneer will have to be cleaned of all old, dried-up glue, and if the veneer is flat this can be done with the toothing plane. As, however, the removal often causes the veneer to become buckled, it is as well to dampen and flat it between two cauls before toothing. When laying the veneer it is also a help to veneer the underside with a plain veneer so that the pull of the one is countered by that of the other. Both can be laid simultaneously with 2 cauls.

The repair of a solid top depends to an extent upon whether it is supported by a carcase as in, say, a chest of drawers, or is entirely self-supporting, as in the leaf of a table.

Warped tops. These are invariably a problem, and sometimes there is no really satisfactory answer, especially if the grain is of a wild and twisted character. It may be possible to reduce the warp by one of the following methods, but possibly some undulation will have to be accepted because too drastic a treatment may easily result in a worse blemish, so that the last state of that thing is worse than the first.

It usually (though not invariably) happens that a top curls upwards at the edges. The probable reason is that wood tends to curl this way towards the light. As a rule, too, the face surface is polished and so sealed, whereas the lower surface is left bare, which allows moisture from the air to enter beneath and so swell the grain. This happens fairly early on and the wood sets more or less permanently in a hollow shape.

It is of little use to damp the hollow side and reverse the top for a few hours. It only resumes its curved shape as it dries out. In any case, the moisture scarcely penetrates through the polish, and the latter is liable to become marked as a consequence of the treatment.

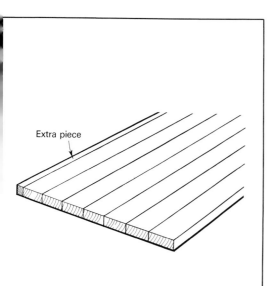

Extra piece

Fig. 1 Top cut into strips and re-jointed.

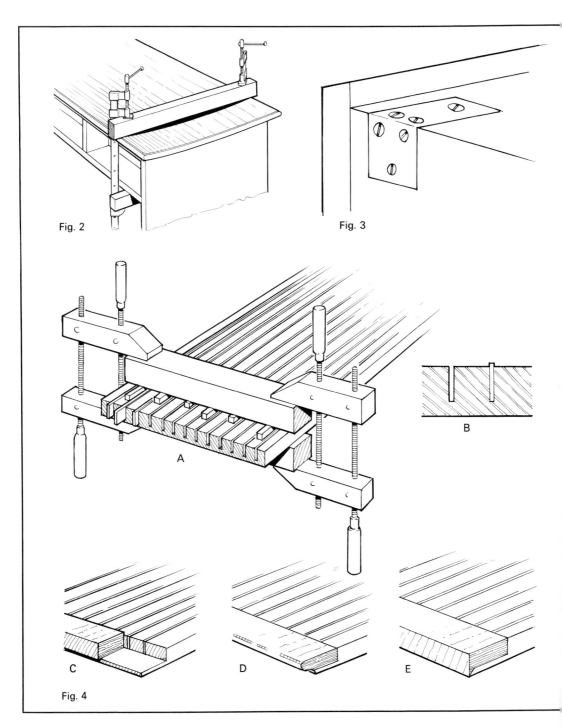

Fig. 2

Fig. 3

A

B

C

D

E

Fig. 4

Fig. 2 Hollow top cramped down with battens. Only possible when the lower framework or carcase is strong.

Fig. 3 Steel bracket recessed and screwed to chest corner to strengthen it.

Fig. 4 A underside of warped top grooved. Note the blocks between the grooves to enable pressure to be applied to the top. Filling strips are shown glued in to the left. **B** grooves sawn to about two-thirds the depth. **C, D, E** treatment at ends of grooves.

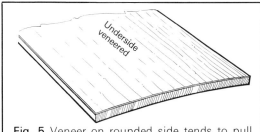

Fig. 5 Veneer on rounded side tends to pull panel flat.

When the top is fixed to a rigid carcase and is not too thick, it is sometimes possible to cramp it down and screw afresh, as in Fig. 2. This, however, is on the assumption that the false top or top rails of the carcase are firmly in position, otherwise the curved top will lift them. In the case of slight curvature, it may be sufficient to remove the loose rails and glue afresh, but the pull of an old top of, say, Cuban mahogany can be great enough to lift even this, if not immediately, after a period of time.

It can be helpful to add a metal bracket in the corner as in Fig. 3. It must be of stout steel, and it is usually necessary to recess it, otherwise it will foul the drawer.

Old hard wood is invariably extremely strong and, in the case of bad warping, it may be necessary to make a series of cuts in the underside as in Fig. 4. These are made about two-thirds the thickness of the wood as at B, and after cramping flat strips of wood are glued in the cuts.

The method is effective if properly done, but calls for some consideration. If the cuts are too deep the wood is liable to show a series of flats, this being especially marked if they are wide apart. A certain amount of experiment is desirable, the cuts being deepened if necessary. A distance of about 18mm.–25mm. (¾in.–1in.) apart is about right. If the spacing is too wide the local bending becomes obvious, whereas when the cuts are close together the bending is more general since the total bend is spread over a greater number of cuts.

The only really practical method of working the grooves is on the circular saw. Generally the plough or the high-speed router cannot be used

because the fence of the tool will not allow it to be used towards the middle of a wide top, unless a batten with straight-edge is cramped to the top to act as a fence. It may be practicable to stop the grooves short at the ends so that they do not show, but with a circular saw the stops would have to be made well short of the ends. This may be enough when the warping is slight, but in a more serious case the grooves will have to be taken right through, and this calls for special treatment at the ends. For a square edge the method at Fig. 4C can be used. A moulded top can have a similar idea as at D, the moulding being worked after fixing. A completely invisible method for a square edge is that at E. The mitre of the applied piece is rather awkward to work owing to the short grain being liable to crumble, but it can be done with care. The main rebate is worked down square first, and the mitre planed with the shoulder plane afterwards.

Having made the cuts, cramp the top flat using battens as in Fig. 4. Note that blocks are used between the grooves to enable the new slips of wood to be inserted. Plane the slips to a finger-tight fit whilst the top is cramped flat and when satisfactory glue the whole. Do not remove the cramps until the glue has thoroughly set. The underside can then be planed. Incidentally, if the top has a joint, do not run a groove right over it.

It is sometimes possible to pull a hollow top flat by laying a sheet of veneer on the underside. The latter must be planed, of course, and the veneer laid with the hammer. The more the latter is worked across the grain, and the more moisture and heat used, the greater the stretching of the veneer, and the greater the subsequent pull and tendency to rectify the curve, Fig. 5.

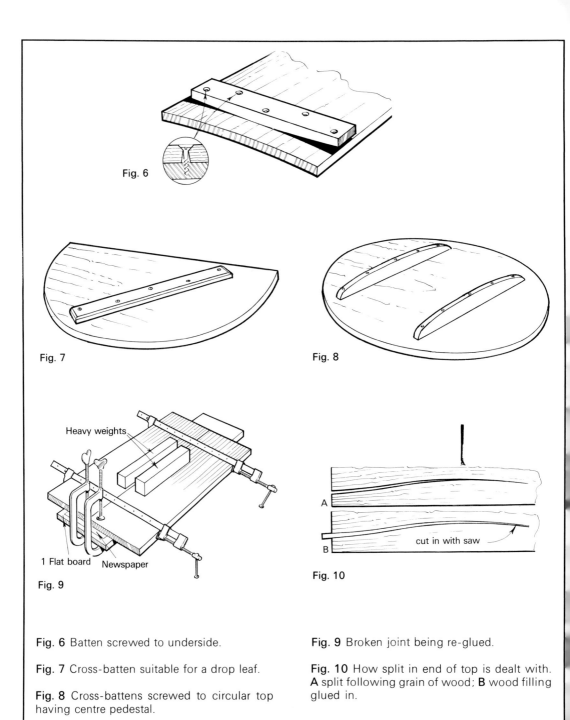

Fig. 6

Fig. 7

Fig. 8

Heavy weights

1 Flat board   Newspaper

Fig. 9

A

B   cut in with saw

Fig. 10

Fig. 6 Batten screwed to underside.

Fig. 7 Cross-batten suitable for a drop leaf.

Fig. 8 Cross-battens screwed to circular top having centre pedestal.

Fig. 9 Broken joint being re-glued.

Fig. 10 How split in end of top is dealt with. A split following grain of wood; B wood filling glued in.

Another method, practicable only when the top has no framework, is to screw one or more battens beneath, as in Fig. 6. If the curvature is fairly severe it is advisable to plane the surface of the batten which faces the wood to a curve in the opposite direction. Otherwise it is doubtful whether the top will be pulled flat unless the batten is very thick. The centre screws can be driven through the normal round hole, but those towards the ends should be pressed through slots so that they do not resist movement.

Sometimes a batten can be screwed on at an angle as in Fig. 7. This is specially useful in the case of, say, a gate-leg table which has a buckled leaf. It will, of course, have to be placed so that it clears the gate. Here again the middle screw can have a normal hole, but those towards the end should have slots rather than round holes to allow for possible movement, though old wood is not likely to move much. A circular table with centre pedestal leg can often have two curved battens screwed on as in Fig. 8.

Broken joints. When joints have failed the only plan is to shoot the joints afresh and re-glue. If care is taken it is possible to avoid planing the surface afterwards, always an advantage when the top is polished. Fig. 9 shows the assembly. The two parts are rubbed together on a flat board with a piece of newspaper interposed and G cramps lightly tightened at the ends. If the top is fairly long or shows any tendency not to be straight along the length, heavy weights are also put in the middle to bring both parts on to the board. Sash cramps are now put on as shown (though in some cases rubbing alone is enough). Be sure to keep the ends level. The glue comes away cleanly later.

Splits. Splits along the grain of the wood as distinct from failed joints require an entirely different treatment. It is useless to rub in glue and cramp together unless the split is only very slight. It will invariably open again as the wood is under considerable stress. The only satisfactory way is to open the split slightly, clean out old polish, wax, etc., and let in a strip of wood which matches the grain of the old as closely as possible.

Fig. 10A shows a wavy split which follows the grain. It should be opened with the saw at the

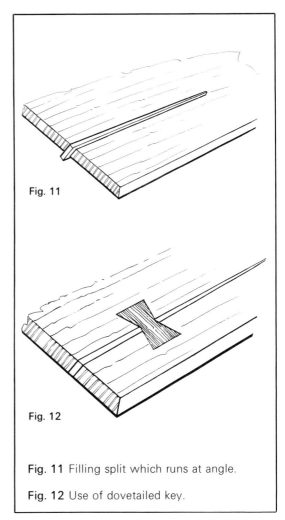

Fig. 11

Fig. 12

Fig. 11 Filling split which runs at angle.

Fig. 12 Use of dovetailed key.

inner or narrow end, and filled with a new piece which is tapered to follow the shape of the split, as at B. It is glued and cramped and levelled later, care being taken not to remove the surface at each side more than can be helped. Sometimes the split is at an angle, as in Fig. 11 and the saw cut will then have to be at the same angle. In this case be careful that the faces are in alignment when cramping as the angle is liable to cause the one piece to rise. Test with the device shown at Fig. 23, page 26. For a really secure job, let a couple of dovetailed keys in at the underside, Fig. 12.

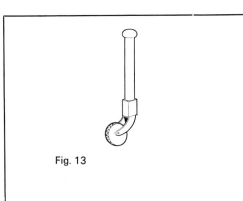

Fig. 13

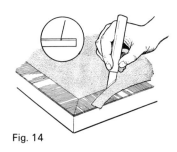

Fig. 14

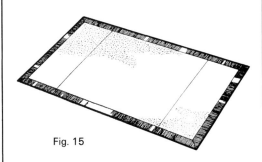

Fig. 15

Fig. 13 Tooling wheel for leather top.

Fig. 14 Undercutting edge of leather. This helps to give a clean butt joint against the veneer surround.

Fig. 15 Leather top in three panels. The joints can be disguised with tooled lines.

Lining a table top. Sometimes the leather top of a writing table has to be re-laid. Usually there is a border all round of veneer, the leather fitting up against this and finishing flush at the top. Hide, morocco or skiver are used.

The old leather is peeled away, the surface cleaned with coarse glasspaper held around a flat block of wood to remove the old adhesive, and any defects should be made good. The adhesive generally used for laying the covering materials is paper-hanger's paste, obtainable in paste or powder form. The latter should be mixed with approximately half the amount of water specified by the manufacturers for paper-hanging in order that a good bond may be obtained.

The tools required for a blind, or plain border are as follows:
1. A tooling wheel obtainable for either a plain line border or with a decorative pattern (Fig. 13).
2. A small piece of linen, to which a little methylated spirit has been added for cleaning the wheel after it has been heated and before it is applied to the covering material. This prevents any discolouration of the material.
3. A suitable brush for spreading the adhesive.

When gluing the leather, stretching may take place, followed by some shrinkage as the glue dries. The leather should therefore be cut full and pressed into the recess with the thumbnail as it dries. Care should be taken when cutting into the recess that the edges are a close fit, and the cutting-in knife should be held at a slight angle to undercut the material. This should avoid any raw edges showing when they are bedded into the recess against the raised surround, Fig. 14. After the covering material has been cut in, the tooling can be commenced. The wheel should be heated over a gas ring or spirit stove and, after wiping clean with the linen, it can be applied to the edges of the covering material with sufficient pressure to form a good impression.

It sometimes happens that the leather available is not large enough to cover the whole surface in one piece and a join becomes necessary. In this event, the surface should be divided into three sections with a large centre panel and two narrower side panels, as shown in Fig. 15, with a close butt joint covered by a tooled line.

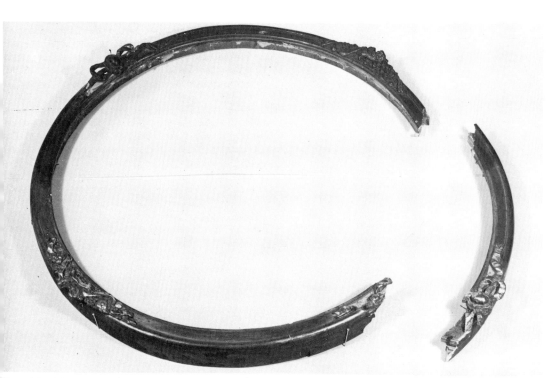

Fig. 16 Gilt mirror frame; with halving joints smashed.

A more elaborate form of tooling can be obtained by the addition of gold leaf. The extra materials necessary are the gold leaf and a camel hair brush or mop. The gold leaf is acquired in tape form with a thin paper backing.

The procedure is exactly the same as for the blind border, except that the gold leaf is used in the tooling. The wheel is heated, as explained for the blind border, and the gold leaf is pressed into the leather. The paper backing is carefully peeled off and the surplus brushed away with the brush or mop. No adhesive of any kind is used to fix the gold leaf to the leather. Should a double line be required, it is advisable to use a straight-edge to guide the tooling wheel in order that a straight line and an even margin be obtained.

Card table top. Card tables are covered with close-woven material similar to billiard table cloth. This resists penetration by the adhesive. The latter should be slow setting, and is usually a good paper-hanger's or book-binder's paste. Sometimes flour paste is used, but in all cases it must be quite thick—more like blancmange—otherwise it is liable to penetrate to the surface. Cut the material about 12·5mm. ($\frac{1}{2}$in.) full all round, and apply the paste to the wood, not the material. Use a piece of hardwood about 127mm. × 38mm. × 6mm. (5in. $1\frac{1}{2}$in. × $\frac{1}{4}$in.) with rounded edges to help in laying.

This is drawn lightly over the surface and any bubbles of air removed. Take special care at the edges to press well down, leaving the surplus overhanging, and leave till the next day before trimming with the knife. Unless this interval is allowed, a gap may show, which is the result of shrinkage.

Chapter eleven

Problems with Veneer

Faults in veneers can range from the simplest blemishes, easily put right, to major troubles such as sometimes occur in marquetry in which the cost of repair may be so excessive that the value of the item may not warrant it. An example of the latter is shown in Fig. 1, a French clock case. All the existing marquetry would have to be lifted and the cost of replacing the missing parts would be so great that, although it was originally a nice clock, the cost of putting it right would be far too high. On the other hand, the clock case in Fig. 2 could be put right, although it would involve a lot of work stripping off old loose veneer and replacing missing parts.

One of the commonest faults that occurs is that of

Fig. 1 French clock case with marquetry. The damage is so extensive that its cost would exceed the value of the case. Damaged marquetry is invariably expensive to repair.

Fig. 2 Clock case the veneer of which is in a bad way, but which could be put right, though involving a great deal of work.

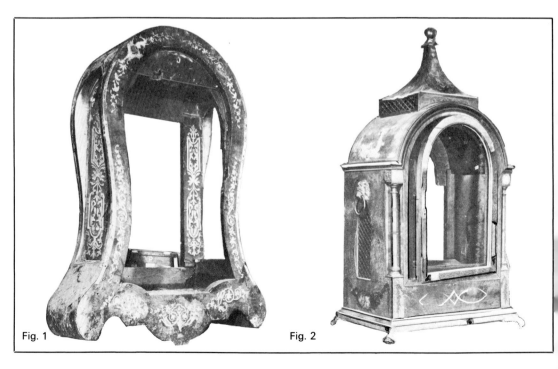

Fig. 1

Fig. 2

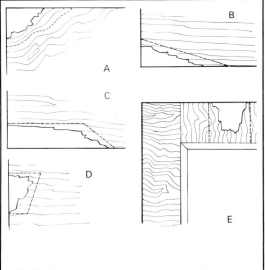

Fig. 3 Damaged corners and edges in veneer. A corner with curly grain; B repair to straight-grained corner; C alternative treatment; D edge repair; E cross-grained framework.

knife-cut veneer to obtain the right thickness. When the core as well as the veneer is damaged the new patch of solid wood can be cut into the groundwork if the grain is suitable. One rule to be followed in all circumstances is to put right any structural fault in the part over which the veneer is laid. All movement in loose joints must be corrected, otherwise the new patch will speedily loosen.

Broken corners. The treatment of a chipped corner or edge depends largely upon the grain of the veneer. If it is of a curly, well-marked type an endeavour should be made to follow it as far as possible, and to select a new patch which matches as closely as it can. Fig. 3A shows the idea. The veneer is cut back with gouges and chisels to follow the general direction of the grain, and the waste eased away.

To make a pattern for the new veneer, a piece of paper is held over the corner and heel ball rubbed over it, thus marking the outline. The new veneer is held in position to give the nearest match of grain and the paper stuck to it. The outline is cut round with a fine fretsaw, and finally trimmed to shape by trial and error with a file. It is useful to keep the paper on because it helps to prevent the veneer from cracking whilst being handled. When ready, glue in position, rubbing down with the back peen of a hammer, and stick gummed tape over the joint to prevent it from opening as the glue dries out. If it tends to lift, a flat block can be warmed and cramped over it with newspaper interposed.

It helps to dampen the face of the veneer, as it prevents the edges from curling upwards. It is, of course, desirable for the new veneer to be slightly thicker than the old so that it can be levelled later without unduly interfering with the surrounding surface. Another advantage is that the block, in being cramped over it, exerts its pressure on the new veneer rather than the old veneer around it.

When the grain of the veneer is straight, one side of the new patch can generally be correspondingly straight, but the end will have to be taken across either square or at an angle. Typical patches are shown at Fig. 3B and C. In the case of a cross-veneered door frame such as that at E it is usually better to cut straight across at both sides, as both joints are in line with the grain and so are less noticeable.

chipped corners and edges. It happens mostly at parts which are handled frequently, or where moving parts create friction, as at door and drawer edges. Drawer rails frequently suffer in this way, especially when the veneer is thin. Much old furniture was better off in this respect, the veneer being sometimes as much as 3mm. ($\frac{1}{8}$in.) thick and was more in the nature of a facing. In all early work the veneer was sawn by hand, and during the Victorian period and the early years of the present century the best veneers were saw-cut by a machine saw rather than sliced by knife. Today it is difficult to buy saw-cut veneer, and the repair of old furniture which originally had saw-cut veneer is sometimes a problem.

It is often necessary to saw veneers by hand or on a circular saw to enable a repair to be completed. Usually the professional finds his supply from oddments left over from odd jobs. Parts may have been dismantled and not used, and sometimes the lower grade Victorian and later items can be cannibalized for the sake of their veneer which was frequently of excellent quality. Alternatively, it may be practicable to use two or more thicknesses of

Drawer rails. Veneered drawer rails frequently suffer, either owing to the drawer itself catching the veneer or because of excessive wear at the ends. Such veneer should be relatively thick—in fact, in many old pieces it was rather a form of facing, often about 3mm. or 5mm. ($\frac{1}{8}$in. or $\frac{3}{16}$in.) thick. Whatever its thickness, it is essential that the worn wood at the back is made good first. This is dealt with in Chapter eight. Not until this is quite sound is any attempt made to repair the veneer. Fig. 17, page 24 shows defects that occur on both the drawer itself and on the main carcase. Usually straight-grained veneer is used on these rails, and the patches are cut in, as shown in Fig. 4, either taken right across or cut in about halfway. Sometimes the grain runs crosswise, notably in walnut furniture, and here the joint is taken right across square. Glue in the patches with overhang all round so that they can be levelled later. Rub down with the hammer or, if necessary, cramp a flat block over the patch with newspaper interposed to prevent it from sticking.

In walnut furniture the veneer is often taken right over a cross-grained edging which projects to form the moulding. An example is that in Fig. 5. When the drawer has received a knock, this strip is often damaged and consequently the veneer has suffered with it. It is essential that the groundwork beneath is made good first, usually involving a new strip of cross-grained walnut being glued in. This is then levelled and a patch of veneer laid, the joints being either shaped or straight in accordance with the grain. Finally the veneer is trimmed at the edges, levelled on the surface and the moulding completed.

Bubbles in veneer. When the veneer has lifted locally in the form of a bubble, it usually implies that the glue beneath has perished. Consequently it is of little use to apply a hot caul over it. It necessitates the introduction of fresh glue. To enable this to be done, a cut must be made through the veneer. Use a thin, keen knife so that the cut is as narrow as possible. A thick knife will compress the edges of the veneer at each side. Follow the grain as closely as possible and make a clean cut through the thickness, Fig. 6. In thick veneer this may mean drawing the knife two or three times along the cut. When the grain is straight it is usually an advantage to cramp a straight-edge over the bubble and work the knife against this.

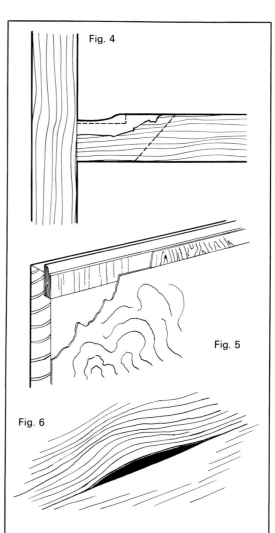

Fig. 4 Veneered drawer rail repair. The framework must be made good before any veneer repair is attempted.

Fig. 5 Veneered drawer front with cross-grained moulding. Here again the groundwork including the wood for the moulding must be repaired first.

Fig. 6 Treatment of bubble in veneer. A cut is made through the veneer with a thin knife to enable fresh glue to be inserted.

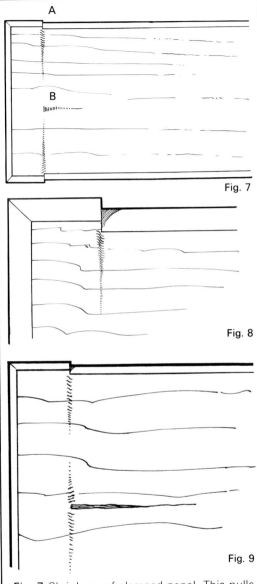

Fig. 7

Fig. 8

Fig. 9

Fig. 7 Shrinkage of clamped panel. This pulls the veneer with it causing stress marks as shown.

Fig. 8 Stress marks in veneer of clamped panel.

Fig. 9 Stress marks and split in veneer.

The cut enables glue to be introduced by a slip of veneer or a thin knife beneath the veneer. A palette knife is excellent, as it is thin and bends easily. If veneer is used, be careful not to let any flakes from it remain under the bubble, as this would prevent the veneer from being pressed down flat. Sometimes rubbing with the cross-peen of the hammer will enable the veneer to be forced down, but usually it is inclined to spring up, and it is necessary to cramp a warm block over the surface with newspaper interposed. It is usually easy to tell whether the veneer is down properly by tapping with the finger nails. A hollow feeling is apparent when the veneer is still raised.

Cracks in veneer. Some cracks in veneer are the result of movement in the groundwork. For instance, wide flush doors and bureau falls in old work were usually made in solid wood, the ends being clamped, or alternatively there might be a flush panel grooved into a framework. Such an item might be anything up to 76cm. (30in.) wide, and it is inevitable that shrinkage will take place. What usually happens is that joints open, and the ends pull in, as in Fig. 7. Animal glue is amazingly adaptable to such movement. Over the years the ends of a panel can pull in about 3mm. ($\frac{1}{8}$in.) or 5mm. ($\frac{3}{16}$in.) and the glue still holds. The veneer is also adaptable up to a point, but so large a movement is bound to show itself in either a complete crack or at least bad stress marks.

The problem is what to do about it. In some cases the cure may by worse than the fault, and it may be better just to accept the blemish. In Fig. 8 the main panel has pulled in some 5mm. ($\frac{3}{16}$in.) and the distortion has exceeded the power of the veneer to stretch, hence the series of cracks along the line of the joint. A cure may be impossible, and in the case of an antique it is left as it is unless there is a clearly defined crack, such as that at Fig. 9. Here a sliver of wood can be let in, but it is extremely unlikely that the figure of the wood will match. It is therefore necessary to tap in the sliver so that a piece of veneer which will match can be inserted. This, however, cannot be done when the veneer is a curl or other decorative wood.

A typical example of the fault I had to deal with was the veneer panel in Fig. 10. The panel was clamped, that is, was tongued to cross-pieces at the ends, the latter running across the grain. The

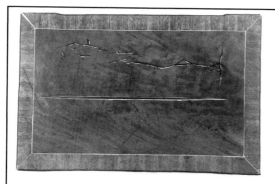

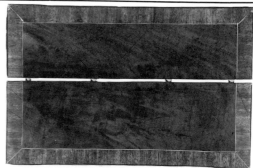

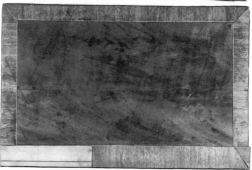

Fig. 10 (above left) Clamped and veneered panel the top jagged cracks are due to shrinkage of the centre panel and the straight is caused by the failure of a joint.

Fig. 11 (above right) The panel cut straight across and dowelled together.

Fig. 12 (below right) The panel nearing completion. Note the width strip added at the bottom corner by new and wider cross-banding.

inevitable had happened: the clamps resisted the shrinkage of the main panel, with the result that one of the joints had opened, breaking the veneer with it, and had caused an ugly, jagged crack in the veneer towards the right-hand clamp. The problem was to put this right in as unnoticeable a way as possible.

As mentioned on page 26, straight or fairly straight cracks can be filled with a sliver, but this was clearly impossible in the present case because the veneer was of curl mahogany and had such pronounced and characteristic grain that it was impossible to match it. I decided, therefore, that the only way was to close up the veneer itself. One method that suggested itself was to lift one part of the veneer up to the crack, make a good joint in the panel and then relay the veneer with a close joint. There was a difficulty, however. Firstly the crack did not reach up beyond the clamps but petered out short of the cross-banding. It would therefore have been necessary to continue the crack right up to the sides. Although this could have been done, there was the further difficulty that the curl was necessarily fragile, and would have been liable to

crack during the lifting process. I therefore decided to cut boldly right through the clamps in line with the crack. This enabled me to re-shoot the joint and obtain a close, clean joint in the veneer. The slight loss of wood in sawdust scarcely affected the grain match.

To give strength and also to ensure that the front surfaces were dead level, I inserted four dowels as shown in Fig. 11. Their positions were squared across the back before separation, and gauged from the front after sawing and shooting. After assembling the joint was almost invisible as in Fig. 12. Of course, there was loss of width in the panel as a consequence, but I made this good at the bottom, stripping away the cross-banding and gluing on a narrow strip of wood. New cross-banding was laid at the bottom, and this had to be slightly wider than the original, but the difference did not show, especially as the new mitres were cut from point to point rather than at 45 deg. as originally. Fig. 12 shows the new widening strip at the bottom; also the new cross-banding partly laid.

The wandering cracks nearer the top needed

92

different treatment. It would have been impossible to make a straight cut across as it would not follow the path of the cracks, and in any case the latter did not extend right to the side. Fortunately, the veneer immediately adjoining the cracks was fairly loose, and I made it as pliable as possible by warming with hot water on a swab. Leaving time for the worst of the moisture to dry out, I then worked in fresh glue through the crack and under the veneer at both sides. By working the cross-peen of the hammer towards the crack from each side it was possible to stretch the veneer and noticeably reduce the width of the crack. A strip of gummed tape over the whole held it whilst the glue set. This left only slight traces of the cracks, and the wider parts I filled in with fine mahogany sawdust mixed with glue. Incidentally, I found that PVA glue was the best to use, as it did not darken the sawdust so much.

Finally I rubbed a piece of half dried-up Wheeler's compound over the fine cracks and left it to harden. Only slight rubbing down was necessary and, after a single rubber of French polish followed by waxing, the defects scarcely showed. In some cases a piece of hard wax suitably coloured can be rubbed over fine cracks. Sometimes I have used Brummer stopping or beeswax melted and coloured with pigment powder to match the wood and with a few flakes of shellac added to harden it. This is applied to the wider cracks with a pointed match-stick whilst molten. It is allowed to heap up slightly and levelled with the chisel when cold. Finally, it is rubbed flat with flour grade glasspaper.

Bruises in veneer. Bruises in a veneered surface can be difficult to deal with in that any attempt to raise the bruise by steaming may result in the veneer being lifted. Unless it is really bad it may be better to leave it as it is. Otherwise it means pricking the surface right through the polish and veneer, putting a damp rag over the place and applying a hot iron so that steam reaches the groundwork and tends to swell it. Unfortunately, apart from the danger of the veneer lifting, the polish may deteriorate, and this will necessitate further treatment.

Lifting veneer. When it is necessary to raise old veneer locally, a soldering iron applied over a damp rag can often be used with advantage. For larger areas, an ordinary flat iron is better. The

polish must usually be removed with a stripper first to enable the damp to penetrate. Use a non-caustic stripper, otherwise the veneer may be darkened. In a difficult case it is helpful to dampen a sheet of foam rubber and leave this on the surface overnight so that the moisture penetrates the veneer. It is usually the start of the lifting at the edges that is the difficulty. Once started, however, a palette knife is handy to pass beneath the veneer, heating the latter locally with the warm soldering iron or a flat iron.

To replace the veneer may be a problem in that it may have become buckled in the lifting process. This necessitates flatting it. A warm, damp rag is passed over the back and as much of the old glue wiped off as possible. It may also be necessary to scrape it. Whilst still damp, the veneer is cramped between two warm, flat cauls and left.

In a really badly crumpled state the veneer may crack under this treatment, and in this case it should be dampened rather more and left between the cauls with a heavy weight on top. In really bad cases it may be necessary to repeat the operation.

Bandings

Inlay bandings. The replacement of inlay bandings may be awkward owing to the difficulty of obtaining an exact match. Originally a wide range of all sizes and woods was available, but this is no longer true. It may be necessary to make up a length. The method varies with the design; usually it is a case of making it in solid blocks and slicing through with a fine saw, unless only a small piece is needed when it can be in veneer. As, however, such bandings are invariably fairly thick (about the same thickness as saw-cut veneer) it is usually necessary to saw up the veneers by hand.

Fig. 13 shows the method of making a banding in solid wood. The core is built up of pieces glued together side by side. The pieces should preferably be sliced on a fine-toothed circular saw so that all are the same thickness. They necessarily show end grain on top and bottom faces. They are glued together on a flat board with paper beneath to prevent their sticking to the board, A. When set, the top surface is skimmed with the plane, the

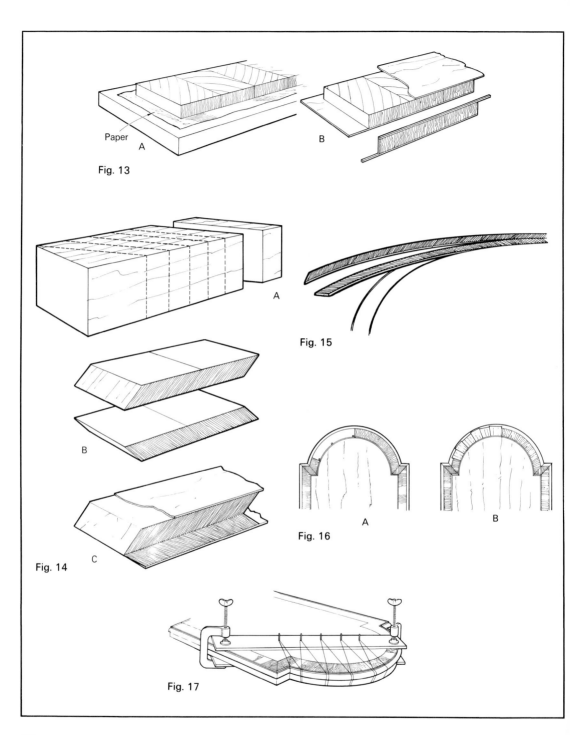

Paper

A

Fig. 13

B

Fig. 14

A

B

C

Fig. 15

Fig. 16

A

B

Fig. 17

whole reversed, the paper removed, and the underside skimmed. A veneer or thin strip is glued to each side as at B, and the whole cramped between flat boards. Finally the bandings are sliced off from the edges as shown, again preferably on a planer circular saw.

Herring-bone banding. This is made in much the same way as in Fig. 14. Strips are cut across the wood at an angle of 45 deg as at A. These are assembled in two lengths, B, and after skimming are glued together and finally sandwiched between two pieces of box or of ebony, C. All other designs are made up on this same principle.

Curved bandings. Sometimes a banding is needed around a curve. In some cases this must be made specially, but when the curve is fairly flat an ordinary straight banding can be separated and bent round providing it is narrow. Fig. 15 shows a narrow herring-bone inlay being inserted in its groove. If it is immediately pressed as it is bent it has the support of the sides of the groove and is less liable to fracture.

In the case of a more acute bend this is not practicable, and it is necessary to make up a curved length. As an example, Fig. 16 shows the method I followed for a door with curved top. It was the waist door of a grandfather clock, and part of the cross-banding was missing. The rebate having been cleaned of dirt and old glue, a boxwood line was first glued and bent round as at A and held to the curve with one or two veneer pins. After an hour or so these pins were removed

Fig. 13 Stages in making cross-banding. A cross-grained blocks glued together; B veneer (light or dark) glued each side and whole sliced through.

Fig. 14 Making a herring-bone inlay. A blocks sliced; B blocks ready for assembly; C whole glued together for cutting up.

Fig. 15 Putting herring-bone around a curve.

Fig. 16 Building up a curved cross-banding. A damaged part cut away and inlay line glued in place; B cross-banding veneer added.

Fig. 17 Fixing inlay string around curve.

and pieces of cross-grained veneer glued round, as at B, being rubbed down with the cross-peen of the hammer, and the joints prevented from opening by gummed tape stuck over them. Once glue had set, the overhang was levelled. As there was a moulding around the curve, I rubbed wax over it to prevent any squeezed-out glue from sticking to it.

When there is also an outer boxwood line, the small rebate for it would be cut with the cutting gauge. To hold the line in position whilst setting, a block with projecting nails is cramped at each side and string taken around the nails, as in Fig. 17. Damping causes the string to tighten.

Sometimes an inlay string is difficult to obtain in the required width and it is necessary to make it specially. The main cutting is done on a fine-toothed circular saw or tenon saw. This alone, however, is not accurate enough, and it is necessary to draw the string through the special gauge shown in Fig. 18. This trims the wood to exact width by the scraping action of the cutter, the wood being held down by the spring. Incidentally,

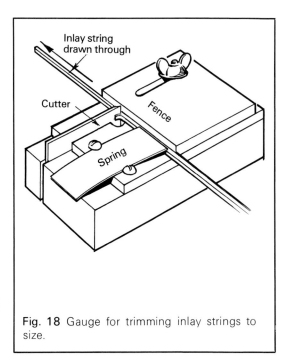

Fig. 18 Gauge for trimming inlay strings to size.

this gauge can also be used to make minute mouldings, the cutter being ground accordingly.

Marquetry

The repair of marquetry can be troublesome, especially when parts are entirely missing, because it is almost impossible to obtain replacements as a standard line to match. They have to be made personally by the repairer, and this can involve a lot of work. Elaborate designs may be beyond the capacity of the repairer, but simple fan corner pieces such as that in Fig. 19 can be made. The tapered pieces are prepared first and fitted together. They are invariably shaded towards one edge, and this is done by holding each individual piece with tweezers and dipping into hot sand, the latter being contained in any suitable metal vessel. It is advisable to experiment on spare pieces first.

They are assembled and a strip of gummed tape stuck over the face. The professional marquetry cutter puts both this assembled fan and the dark parts together and cuts through both with a fine fretsaw. Probably for one odd repair this is not worthwhile and it is quicker to cut the series of hollows around the edge with a keen gouge and fit pieces of veneer up to them as at Fig. 19C.

Again, gummed tape or newspaper is stuck over the face and when set the outer edge is trimmed to the quadrant shape. Finally a boxwood or ebony line is fitted up around the curve, the marquetry being held down by a block cramped over it, and the inlay line bent around, glued, and held by veneer pins driven in at the side of the outer edge. When complete it is fitted and glued down as a whole.

Sometimes marquetry panels have been lifted in parts, often with little pieces missing. The treatment can be a time-consuming operation. If only parts are missing it involves fitting replacements, the outline being obtained by rubbing heel ball on tracing paper held over the work. The paper is then stuck to new veneer and the outline sawn round or cut with a sharp, pointed knife. Note that the paper stiffens the veneer and helps to avoid cracking. Each part is then finally fitted to the recess and glued down. It should stand slightly proud so that it can be levelled afterwards.

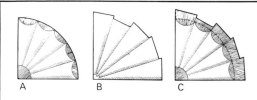

Fig. 19 Stages in making marquetry fan.

When marquetry has lifted badly in places the treatment may be difficult. The cramping of a hot caul over the raised part can be tried, but usually the glue beneath has perished and if possible fresh glue should be worked in. This is usually possible when the bubble is at the edge, or when one of the pieces of marquetry has come adrift, the glue being worked in with a palette knife.

When the bubble is a small local one it is usually possible to remove one of the pieces of veneer either entirely or sufficiently for fresh glue to be inserted, care being taken to see that it is replaced in the same way as before. It sometimes happens, however, that a large area has come adrift, and the satisfactory plan is to raise the whole, clean off the old glue, and lay afresh. The method depends largely upon the size of the job.

Small areas can usually be lifted by putting a damp rag over the surface and using an iron to warm the glue and so liquefy it. It is, however, necessary to remove the polish first as damp cannot penetrate through this. One corner of the veneer is lifted, a chisel inserted, and the veneer gradually eased up, little by little, the iron being kept just ahead of the chisel. An electric soldering iron is convenient for work of this kind, the heat being kept as low as will just soften the glue. It is a rather tricky business, and it is as well to keep pieces of gummed tape handy to stick over the veneer as it is raised so that the pieces of marquetry are kept in the right position. The old glue is removed and the marquetry laid afresh. If, however, it is not flat or if the parts have got out of position, they should be manoeuvred into the correct place and pieces of gummed tape stuck over the face. It may then be necessary to flat the whole by cramping between two flat cauls. When cramping down afresh it is invariably necessary to put a couple of veneer pins in unnoticeable positions, otherwise the whole is liable to float since the glue becomes liquid when it is heated.

Brass inlay often causes complications when a solid groundwork shrinks across the grain. The brass, when in the form of a line, is unable to accommodate itself to the reduced size and lifts, forming a small loop. It is impossible to press this down as it is, because the groove is too short for the brass. The only plan is to cut across the inlay with a fine hacksaw or metal-cutting fretsaw.

Generally the saw kerf removes enough to enable the parts to be pressed down, but if necessary the ends can be filed still more. Old dirt and grease must be cleaned out as far as possible with a narrow chisel or the edge of a bradawl. Generally the brass is springy, so that it is necessary to cramp a block over the inlay whilst the glue sets. If Scotch glue is used it should be made up fresh. Some recommend the addition of garlic to the glue to increase its grip; others prefer to add a little Venice turpentine. A better alternative is to use two-part Epoxy resin (see page 109).

Sometimes the spring of the metal is so great that it is unwise to rely purely on the adhesive. Matters can be helped by drilling fine holes at intervals about the size of a household pin and tapping in brass pins. The latter can, in fact, be pins with the heads cut off and the lower end filed to a slightly tapered shape so that it grips the brass as it is driven home. If the groundwork is of really hard wood, do not attempt to drive in the pins without pre-boring. For the latter I generally use a needle with the point nipped off and the end filed straight across to form an edge.

Sometimes parquetry panels lift, and can cause trouble when extensive. Small bubbles can often be pressed down with a warm caul, but generally the glue beneath has perished. This necessitates carefully removing one of the pieces of veneer to enable fresh glue to be worked in. If the veneer tends to crack when the block is pressed down, it is advisable to warm it first with a hot rag before using the warm caul. One of the difficulties is the liability of the replaced veneer to shift. It should therefore be held with a piece of gummed tape stuck over the whole.

Really large areas of lifted parquetry or marquetry are difficult to deal with and may necessitate a hot caul being pressed over the entire surface to soften the glue. First, however, either gummed tape should be stuck over the inlay or a piece of thin brown paper glued over it to hold the parts together. It is a difficult operation and best avoided if possible.

Chapter twelve

Mechanical Joints

These include moving parts of all kinds. Obviously they are liable to wear, and their repair poses special problems.

Rule joints. Although usually reliable, the rule joint found on some gate-leg tables, Fig. 1, can sometimes cause trouble, the most usual fault being that of binding. The correct arrangement is that in Fig. 2, from which it will be seen that the hinge centre is embedded in the wood from beneath and is vertically beneath the square of the moulded section. This, of course, necessitates the use of special hinges which have the countersinking of the screw holes on the reverse side from the knuckle. The point about this is that, apart from its neat appearance, the moulded shape sustains the weight when the leaf is in the up position, whereas in the plain square-edged joint the hinges take all the strain. Yet another feature is that when the leaf is lowered there is no gap at the edge since the tip of the hollow member always covers the bottom of the round, Fig. 2B. Lastly there is no projecting knuckle at the underside.

Shrinkage is no problem in the rule joint, but swelling of the wood through dampness can cause binding. Consider Fig. 3, which is a section through the joint. The distance between the screws shown by the arrow is clearly fixed by the metal of the hinge, and if the wood swells it is inevitable that the parts will bind against each other.

In such a case the best remedy is to leave the parts in a dry atmosphere for as long as possible to enable moisture to dry out. Drying is speeded up if the parts are separated, and if the round portion has been french polished or varnished it is helpful to rub it down with fine glasspaper held on a wood rubber shaped to a reverse of the moulding. Otherwise the moisture is trapped in and cannot be got rid of easily.

Once the rule joint has been properly made and hinged it is seldom that anything goes wrong with it, except binding due to moisture as just outlined. It does occasionally happen, however, that fresh hinges have been fitted at some time, or that old damaged hinges have to be replaced. It is important that these must be of a size to bring the knuckle

Fig. 1 Gate-leg table with pivoted gates, and top with rule joints.

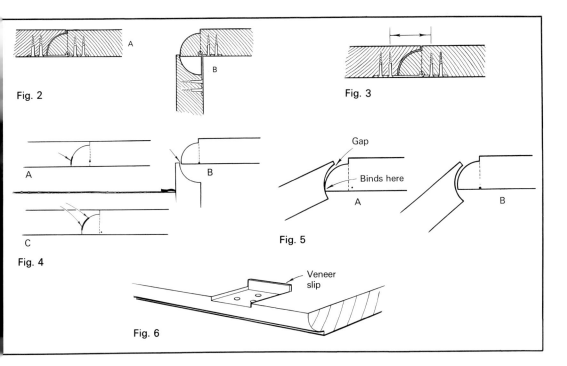

Fig. 2

Fig. 3

A

B

Fig. 4

A

B

C

Fig. 5

Gap

Binds here

A

B

Veneer slip

Fig. 6

Fig. 2 Section through rule joints. This shows the hinge correctly positioned.

Fig. 3 Rule joint section. Distance shown by arrow is controlled by hinge screws; any swelling of wood will cause binding.

Fig. 4 Faults in hinge position. **A** centre too high. Binds at arrow as leaf is lowered; **B** centre too low. Shows gap at arrow when leaf is lowered. **C** centre too far in. Binds at arrows.

Fig. 5 Faults in hinge position. **A** centre too far in; **B** centre too low.

Fig. 6 Veneer to prevent hinge moving inwards when screwing.

centres into the correct position. Fig. 4 and 5 show some of the troubles that can arise when the centre is not in the correct position. Note that this centre must be vertically beneath the top square of the moulding, and that it must be recessed in from beneath. If sunk in too far it will cause binding; if

too low will show a gap along the edge when the leaf is lowered.

One of the difficulties of fitting new hinges is that of the screw holes. If the positions are markedly different there is usually no bother as new ones are bored. However, if they are only a little out it is awkward to bore new holes close to the old ones.

Plugging the old holes and making new ones may sometimes be successful, but in bad cases it is better to fill in the old recesses and start off from scratch, cutting fresh ones to suit the new hinges.

If the old recesses are used and the holes are not exactly in the right positions it is occasionally helpful to insert a slip of veneer or thin wood at one side or at the ends, as in Fig. 6, as it helps to prevent the hinge from being dragged out of position. When repairs and any polishing are completed it helps to rub a piece of candle grease over the moving parts.

Occasionally the cure of a fault turns out to be extremely simple. I was asked to look at a gate-leg

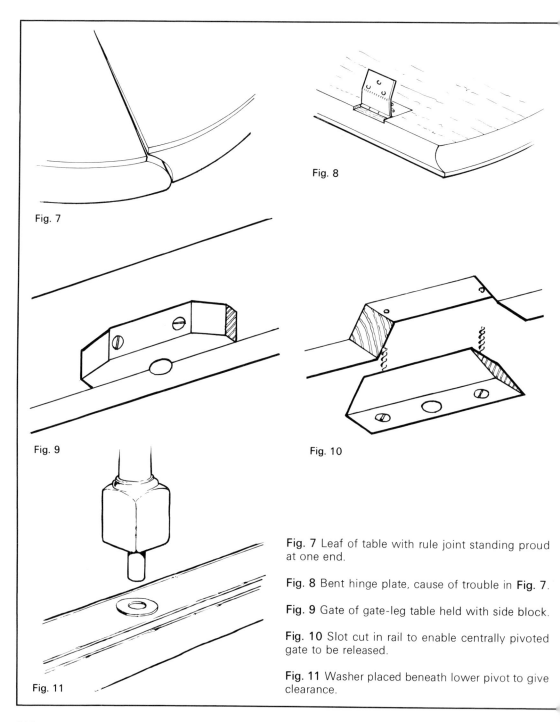

Fig. 7

Fig. 8

Fig. 9

Fig. 10

Fig. 11

Fig. 7 Leaf of table with rule joint standing proud at one end.

Fig. 8 Bent hinge plate, cause of trouble in **Fig. 7**.

Fig. 9 Gate of gate-leg table held with side block.

Fig. 10 Slot cut in rail to enable centrally pivoted gate to be released.

Fig. 11 Washer placed beneath lower pivot to give clearance.

table, the leaf of which was protruding above the main top at one end by about 3mm. ($\frac{1}{8}$in.) as shown in Fig. 7. There seemed no obvious reason why it should have happened suddenly. On enquiry, it appeared that children had been playing in the room. Examination showed that the end hinge, and to a lesser extent the middle one, had been bent, probably the result of something being jammed between the leg and the leaf and the latter pushed inwards. The plate of the hinge was thus bent as in Fig. 8, with the result that the leaf showed a gap when in the down position and stood proud when raised. The cure was obvious.

Another fault that occurs sometimes in a gate-leg table is that the pins or dowels on which the gates are pivoted become worn with continuous use, or even break off. Their replacement is a simple matter when the main framework of the table can be dismantled, because the gates can be freed and fresh dowels bored in. Often these old tables were not assembled with glue, the joints being held with pegs driven through them and they can thus be taken apart easily. It may be, however, that the frames have been glued, possibly during a repair job in order to stiffen them, and it is thus difficult to free the gates, though it depends upon the particular way the table was made.

Occasionally one comes across the arrangement in Fig. 9 in which a block is screwed to one side of the top rail, the dowel hole being bored centrally between the two as shown. Replacement is simple, as removal of the block frees the gate at the top. This, however, is unusual in an old table, the hole generally being bored in the middle of the top rail, which of course necessitates the gate being inserted during the assembly of the main framework. When the latter cannot be taken apart it is usually necessary to cut a notch in the underside of the top rail as in Fig. 10, enabling the gate to be withdrawn. The dowel in the gate having been renewed, a new block is fitted to the notch. It is slipped over the dowel, the whole pushed into position, and the block screwed. I have always found it an advantage to fit and screw the block first independently of the gate. It makes the fixing so much simpler than when the gate is in position, because it is much easier to use the bradawl. When the gate is fitted the screws are put in without difficulty as the holes have already been made.

Quite often a gate is liable to drop when opened owing to excessive wear at the pivots. It is usually a help to slip a washer over the dowel at the bottom as in Fig. 11. Make sure, however, that the gate fits in both the open and closed positions.

Hinge problems. Hinging faults in doors, falls, etc., can arise from various causes. One of the commonest troubles is that of binding. Either the door will not close, or it springs open. The usual cause is that the screws are too big so that the heads foul each other when the door is closed, Fig. 12A. It often happens over the years that the screws have been withdrawn and replaced several times, and if they are overtightened the thread is stripped so that the screws fail to hold. To get over this a larger size of screw is used, with the result that the heads project and prevent the hinge from closing. The only way is to deepen the countersinking with the rose countersink so that the screws go in flush, or plug the holes and bore afresh. It may be that forcing the door to close over the years has bent the plate of the hinge, and it is necessary to remove it from the door and hammer it flat on a block of metal.

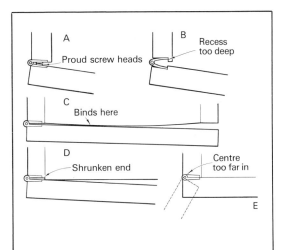

Fig. 12 Causes of binding when hinging. A screw heads project; B hinge strained by over-deep recesses; C rounded carcase front prevents door from closing; D end has shrunk leaving top and bottom proud; E door cannot open freely.

Another cause of binding is due to the recesses being too deep, Fig. 12B. It may be that at some time the hinges have been replaced with thinner ones. This can usually be corrected by inserting a slip of veneer or thick paper in the recess beneath the hinge, but it is a mistake to pack out unnecessarily.

It can sometimes happen, possibly due to movement in the wood or to unskilful treatment at some time, that the front edge of the cupboard is rounded, as at Fig. 12C. It is clear that the door is liable to spring open, and the only plan is to plane the wood true. A similar case can arise when the cabinet end has shrunk but not the top or bottom, D. Here again, planing is the only answer.

Sometimes it is the closing edge of a door which is tight, or the meeting edges of a pair of doors. This is usually due to the joints having given so that the door is wider than normal, and re-gluing and cramping will correct it.

It may be, however, that the joints are still holding although the shoulders may be slightly open. Animal glue is a curious substance and quite considerable movement can take place over the years with little effect on its holding power. In any case, it might be awkward to disturb an elaborate door with tracery or other detail. If it is quite sound, the simplest way is to accept the condition and, if necessary, fill in any gap at the shoulders. The edge can then be eased.

When a door has wide stiles it is possible that the overall width may be increased owing to swelling, the result of dampness. Here the repairs should be left in a dry atmosphere for as long as possible to enable any dampness to dry out. This may put things right. Otherwise easing the edge is the only answer.

Centre hinges. These are usually free from binding troubles except when caused by distortion of the carcase, such as that in Fig. 13. It does sometimes happen, however, that the seating on the bottom hinge is badly worn or, if there is no seating, the washer is missing. It will be realized that one or the other is needed to give clearance to the bottom of the door, Fig. 14. Either a new hinge is needed or a washer must be slipped over the pin. At the top no seating is needed. Incidentally, when centre

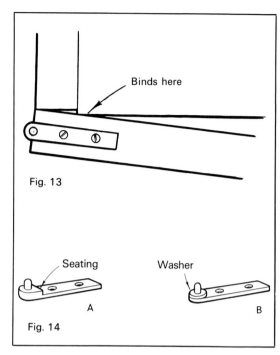

Fig. 13

Binds here

Seating

Washer

A

B

Fig. 14

Fig. 13 Centre hinge binding caused by top being proud.

Fig. 14 Alternative bottom centre hinges. Top hinge needs neither seating nor washer.

hinges are used there is usually a loose top member or a loose plinth or stand. The removal of either will leave the door free, and this is something to keep in mind when taking a job to pieces. The unthinking removal of a top may leave the door free to fall outwards and so cause a smash.

One possible cause of scraping is that the screws have become loose and have worked out so that the heads are proud. The fact that one at least of the screws enters the end grain of the stile renders this specially likely to happen, because screws do not hold in end grain. The use of longer screws will usually put this right.

Knuckle joints. These are used to pivot the legs of drop-leaf and card tables, or for hinged bearers, Fig. 15. They stand up to wear extremely well, but the effect of excessive wear is to render the joint

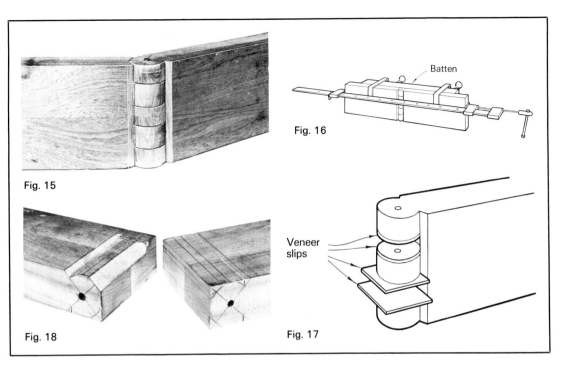

Fig. 15

Fig. 16

Fig. 18

Fig. 17

Batten

Veneer
slips

Fig. 15 Knuckle joint for swing leg or flap. Strong and hard-wearing mechanical joint.

Fig. 16 Cramping knuckle joint for re-boring.

Fig. 17 Bearing surfaces packed out with veneer.

Fig. 18 Two parts of the knuckle joint in process of being worked.

loose. It is difficult to carry out any effective repair once the joint is badly worn because it relies on its rubbing surfaces for rigidity, not merely the centre metal pin. Matters can be helped by fixing a flat batten to one side with thumbscrews to bring the parts into alignment and to hold them straight whilst a cramp is tightened over the length, as in Fig. 16. The metal rod (usually 6mm. ($\frac{1}{4}$in.) diam.) is knocked out, and the hole enlarged by 1·5mm. ($\frac{1}{16}$in.) using a morse drill or shell bit if the right size is available. A new 7mm. ($\frac{5}{16}$in.) iron rod is then tapped in. This will stiffen the joint for a further period of service, but in the nature of things it will not be so strong as when all the surfaces are bearing properly.

When the parts are really loose, a more drastic treatment is that in Fig. 17. The bearing surfaces of one piece are pared down flat and slips of veneer glued on to them. When the glue has set, the edges are levelled, and the other piece similarly pared until it makes a fairly tight fit. The parts are then assembled and the pivoting hole enlarged by 1·5mm. ($\frac{1}{16}$in.) as before. The only alternative is to make a new knuckle joint with short members and splice or halve on to the existing rails. In the case of worm-eaten wood (beech was often used for such rails, and worms love it) there is no option but complete new rails with fresh knuckle joints. Fig. 18 shows a knuckle joint in the process of being worked.

A similar type is the finger joint in Fig. 19. It is not so neat as the knuckle but is often found on old pieces. The general repair is much the same. Fig. 20 shows how the parts work.

Extending tables. A type widely found is the draw-extension, Fig. 21, in which the leaves are raised to the level of the main top when pulled out. The latter lifts during the process, and drops down

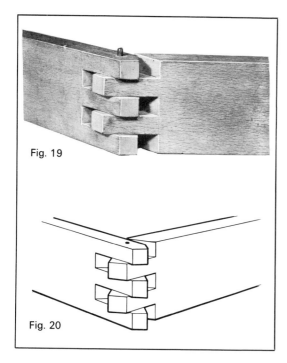

Fig. 19

Fig. 20

again to normal height when the leaf is right out. The leaves are supported by tapered bearers which run in notches cut in the underframe. After extensive use the rubbing surfaces become worn, and the leaves tend to drop when pulled out, as in Fig. 22. Depending on circumstances the wear can be made good either by inserting a new bearing surface in the notch or on the bearer. The former is obviously the simpler, but will not necessarily put things right, because, although it may be correct in one position, it may not be so in the other. The only plan is to fit a temporary slip in the notch and try the effect. If in order, a new block can be fitted and glued in. Do not merely put in a piece of veneer because, even though it is thick enough, it will soon wear away. In bad cases the bearers

Fig. 19 Finger joint for swing leg or flap. This is a cheaper alternative to the knuckle joint.

Fig. 20 Details of finger joint.

Fig. 21 (below) Draw-extension table showing bearers. At **X** bearers tapered so that leaf is raised to level of main top when withdrawn; notches at **Y**.

have to be either made good or renewed, especially if they have become bent owing to extensive use with the leaves pulled out, Fig. 23.

Tables with telescopic extending action are not often found, but troubles that arise with them are usually due to dampness which causes swelling in the slides and bearers. In the most satisfactory method the whole of the bearing action is separated and left for as long as possible to dry out. As a rule, prime quality birch was used for these Victorian tables and the workmanship was first rate.

Generally, then, the fault is that of the conditions. At any rate, one should be cautious before easing the slides because if loose the table will sag. Test the individual parts when any dampness has dried out, and rub the bearing surfaces with a piece of candle grease. Sometimes the trouble is due to tie bars having become loose, and the re-fixing of these puts things right. Remember, in any case, that the slides were invariably made slightly curved along their length so that when the table was fully extended any sag in the middle was cancelled out.

Pedestal tables. Circular tables with centre pedestal were frequently made to tilt and the top was usually pivoted on stout dowels worked in the top wood plate fixed to the pedestal top with a through-mortise and tenon joint. Continuous wear

Fig. 22 Results of wear in notch of draw-table.

Fig. 23 Bent bearer causing leaf to drop.

Fig. 24 (bottom) Top of tripod pedestal with pivoting dowels renewed.

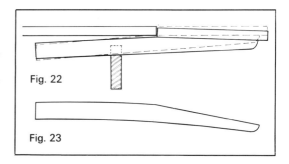

Fig. 22

Fig. 23

causes the dowels to become worn—they may even be broken off. Fig. 24 shows how the dowels can be renewed. It is of no use to replace them individually at each side because the holes in the top plate would practically emerge at the rounded corners. The only way is to fit a new, square piece right across the plate as shown. The dowels at the ends are centred and a circle of the dowel size drawn in with dividers. The shape is then carefully pared down with the chisel, the shoulder being sawn first. The whole is glued into a rebate cut in the plate and the edge rounded afterwards. I generally use resin glue for the purpose.

It frequently happens that the holes in the rails have also become worn, and this may necessitate new rails. It is advisable to bore these holes first because the dowels have to be cut to the size of the bit used for boring. It can be annoying having cut the dowels to find that you have no bit of the right size!

Since the holes in the rails practically emerge at the edge there is the danger that the bit may break out. The answer is to mark the position with square and gauge and hold the two rails together in the vice when boring as in Fig. 25. Thus the one rail supports the other.

Fig. 25 Boring holes near edge of top rails.

Chapter thirteen

Adhesives

The traditional adhesive for woodwork is Scotch glue which is still widely used in the antique repair trade. Excellent if properly prepared and used, its chief drawback is that it is not resistant to damp, but this generally does not matter for furniture.

American brand equivalents for several adhesives are given in brackets.

Preparing Scotch glue. It can be obtained in cake, pearl or powder form. Of these the last two are the more easily and quickly prepared, but all make exactly the same glue in the end. If cake glue is used it must be broken up into small pieces inside a piece of sacking to prevent fragments flying about. The pieces are put into the glue pot, covered with water, and left overnight. Pearl or powder glue is immersed in the same way. Note that the container must be either tinned or of copper, as a rusty iron pot causes discoloration. If a proper pot is not available a jam-jar can be used in a saucepan of water as in Fig. 1. The glass will not crack if the level of the glue is kept above that of the water in the saucepan, but a slip of wood is placed beneath the jar to avoid contact with the saucepan. It must be heated from the cold. To plunge the jar into hot water would inevitably cause cracking.

Glue should never be boiled. The optimum temperature is in the region of 60 deg C (140 deg F), no hotter. There is no need to test it with a thermometer, but a rough guide is to remember that the hottest water used for washing the hands is about 49 deg C (120 deg F), and the glue is certainly hotter than this but is nowhere near boiling heat.

It will be found that after being steeped all night in cold water the glue has settled into a thick mass, and should be stirred with a stick from time to time as it is heated. To test for consistency raise the brush a little way above the pot when the glue is hot. It should run down into the pot in a continuous stream, free from lumps, yet without breaking into drops. It is best when fresh, and for an important job it is advisable to make up a new supply. Today it is felt that repeated re-heating causes loss of strength. It is interesting to note, however, that Sheraton in his *Cabinet Dictionary* says that 'old glue is best and its goodness and strength increases by frequent boiling if it be not burnt!'

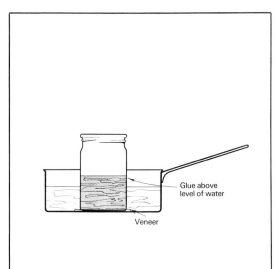

Glue above
level of water

Veneer

Fig. 1 Heating Scotch glue in jar. A slip of veneer or thin wood beneath the jar avoids contact with the hot metal of the saucepan.

A proprietary animal glue such as *Croid Aero* is excellent and, being in jelly form, has only to be heated. Another proprietary glue is *Fortil* and is used similarly to the above. For those who prefer a cold-application glue there is *Croid Universal*, *(Contact cement)*, but even this requires to be warmed in cold weather.

Using animal glue. With all hot glues it is important that the work is heated before the glue is applied. Unless this is done the glue is chilled by the cold wood and loses much of its strength. Furthermore, the assembly time is reduced since gelling takes place quickly. Any form of heat can be used—gas ring, electric fire, open fire, etc., but when a flame is used it is important that the edges and corners are not scorched, as this causes a black joint line.

The work needs to be gone about fairly speedily, including testing for squareness, etc., as well as cramping. For an elaborate job it is therefore advisable to have assistance. All cramps should be opened the right amount beforehand, softening blocks ready to hand, and testing apparatus placed ready. Although initial setting is fairly rapid as the glue loses heat, subsequent hardening is slow, and cramps should be left overnight.

Animal glue is invariably used for veneering—in fact, for hammer veneering it is the only glue that can be used. Modern shops use resin glue for press veneering, but this is seldom done in the antique trade.

Resin glue. This has many virtues and is invaluable on occasion. It is extremely strong, sets fairly quickly (the rate can be varied), the type normally available is used cold, is stain-free (if precautions are taken), and is highly damp-resistant. As against this, it cannot be re-liquefied once it has set and, although in most cases this may not matter, it does mean that the work has to be done accurately as no correction can be made later. It is for this reason that its use in veneering is not recommended unless proper cramping appliances are available. In any case, it cannot be used in hammer veneering.

One form of resin glue is in the form of a syrup which remains liquid until brought into contact with a water-like hardener, whereupon hardening begins straight away. In the case of mortise and tenon and similar joints, the usual plan is to put the syrup in the mortise, and the hardener on the tenon. Thus the assembling of an elaborate job is simplified in that setting does not begin until the parts are brought together. Iron, such as the ferrule of a brush, should be avoided as this may cause discolouration. A glue of this type is *Aerolite 300 (Boat Armor Epoxy Resin)*.

The only drawback of this glue is that its shelf life is limited. Depending upon temperature, this is in the region of three months, after which it becomes rubbery and useless. This may be awkward for the small user, and for this reason the same glue is available in powder form, requiring only the addition of water to convert it into the normal syrup, *Aerolite 306 (Boat Armor Epoxy Resin)*. The powder glue, if stored properly and sealed, keeps for two years or more. Another type of powder glue has the hardener incorporated in it, *Cascamite (Secur-It or Tight-Bond)* waterproof glue. Setting begins as soon as water is added, though there is ample time for assembling.

A feature common to all these resin glues is that heat accelerates setting, and advantage of this can sometimes be taken by warming the work after assembling, thus enabling cramps to be released for other work.

Casein glue. This is not widely used today, and seldom for repair work. It has the advantage of cold application, but is liable to stain some hardwoods. Thus any penetration through veneer is almost certain to cause discoloration, and even simple joints may show marking, especially if surplus is not wiped off immediately. One other point is that, although it is strong when set, it has no natural tackiness, so that it is not practicable to rub joints together as when animal glue is used. Cramping is necessary, and cramps should be left on until complete setting has taken place. It is not possible to use the hammer for veneering.

Polyvinyl-acetate (PVA), *(Poly-urethane).* This is a relatively recent product and is used cold. Most modern types have a resin additive. It is a fairly thick white liquid used just as it is but, although free from staining, may turn a dark brown colour when brought into contact with some woods. This does not matter with dark woods, but may be objectionable in some light timbers. Joints must be cramped. One feature of some makes is that, although strong when set, they are liable to creep. Thus a joint subject to stress in one direction may tend to sag eventually, although it may appear as strong as ever. For the general run of such joints as the mortise and tenon which is mechanically strong in itself there is no difficulty. Perhaps the best way of exemplifying the characteristic is that if a heavy panel were held to the wall purely by Polyvinyl-acetate glue, it slowly descends.

Rubber-based adhesives. In repair work these are used occasionally for items to which it is difficult to apply cramps. An instance is that of elaborately carved detail, the shape of which renders cramping impossible. Scotch glue if held for a minute or two will hold the parts together if they are light, but heavy ornament is liable to drop off. The advantage of a contact adhesive is that, after coating both parts and leaving partially to set, it immediately grabs when the two are brought together and holds firmly. A thin coating should be given, otherwise a glue line will show. Only plain butt joints can be made. Parts which slide together such as tenons, tongues, etc. are impossible because the glue grips before the parts can be pressed home.

Contact adhesive is occasionally useful for veneering shaped work, especially in cases where it would be difficult to make a reverse caul or use a sandbag. Since the grab is immediate, however, it needs exact positioning of the veneer as it is almost impossible to shift the veneer once it is placed on the groundwork, though some adhesives such as *Thixofix (Epoxy)* are better in this respect in that slight adjustment can be made if done immediately. To get best results I apply a coat to both groundwork and veneer and allow both to dry out completely. I then give a second coat, leave until touch dry, then place the veneer in position.

Sometimes when material other than wood has to be glued, special adhesives are required.

Metal inlay. Underside of inlay should be scored to give a grip. Freshly-made Scotch glue is effective with garlic added when hot. An alternative is a little plaster of Paris added to the glue. Some men recommend the use of a spoonful of Venice turpentine to a pot of hot glue. Personally I prefer to use one of the two-part epoxy resin glues.

Incidentally, when a brass inlay is used across the grain of a wide panel, shrinking will often cause lifting since the brass does not shrink with the wood. It is necessary to shorten the brass line by sawing straight across and filing (if need be). Usually it is kinked, and to straighten it a reasonable length will have to be lifted to enable it to be laid on a metal plate so that it can be beaten flat. If badly kinked it may be quicker to insert a complete new length. Often it is necessary to cramp a flat block over the repair as the brass is liable to spring up. Newspaper should be placed beneath the block to prevent it from sticking.

When pieces of fretted brass are missing it is necessary to fret out new pieces to replace them. To obtain the shape a piece of paper should be placed over the part and rubbed with heel ball or a lead pencil so that the outline is marked. This is stuck over the brass and the latter fretted out. These brass repairs are invariably awkward, and can be time-consuming.

Celluloid, ivory. Score the underside to provide a key but, if it is semi-transparent, rub on fine glass-paper instead as coarse marks may show through. Use freshly-made Scotch glue with garlic added, or use *Durofix*. Or apply contact adhesive thinly.

Tortoiseshell. Roughen the underside with Fine 2 glasspaper, and use fresh Scotch glue, resin or polyvinyl. If it is buckled, steep in warm vinegar to make it pliable. Depending upon the particular job, it may be necessary to add vermilion pigment to the glue to colour it red, or flake white to lighten.

Baize and leather. Use paperhanger's paste mixed to double strength. If too much water is used it may tend to penetrate. Fish glue can also be used, but is much more expensive. If it is used it should be left to dry for a few minutes to avoid penetration.

Rubber to wood. Not often wanted, but occasionally needed in cushioning. Use one of the rubber-based contact adhesives. Usually the surfaces are allowed to dry or become tacky before use, but follow the instructions on the container.

Plastics to wood. Either a rubber-based contact adhesive can be used, or one of the synthetic resins. For small odd parts—inlays, etc.—use *Durofix* or *Seccotine*.

Chapter fourteen

Effects of Damp, Woodworm and Central Heating

It sometimes happens that a piece of furniture has been stored in a damp cellar or outhouse and requires attention. The usual faults that manifest themselves are: drawers and doors which stick or bind, table leaves and any similar moving parts which are stiff, rusted hinges and screws, lifted and buckled veneer, swollen timber, failure of glued parts generally, and dull and deteriorated finish. Wood is a hygroscopic substance which gives up its moisture during the seasoning process, but equally absorbs it if placed in a damp atmosphere. Just as giving up moisture causes shrinkage across the grain, so absorbing it results in swelling, hence the troubles outlined.

Damp furniture

As a rule the absorption of damp is a fairly slow process, made still slower by the finish of the item, this acting as a barrier. Movement in the wood is thus quite slow, and any attempt at putting things right should also be slow because speeding up by heat only results in all sorts of other troubles. For instance, animal glue has the curious quality of being able to adapt itself to slow movement and still retain its grip. Thus in a clamped door a panel can shrink as much as 6mm. ($\frac{1}{4}$in.) or so across a width of 38·1cm. (15in.) so that it stands in about 3mm. ($\frac{1}{8}$in.) at each side, although the glue still grips. Fig. 1 shows the corner of a clamped panel of the type often found on a bureau fall in which the movement can be seen clearly. Sometimes there is a surrounding inlay banding or line, and this frequently adapts itself to the movement without breaking.

If, however, the movement is speeded up, as it would be if the work were brought into a hot room and left there, the glue would probably fail straight away, resulting in loose joints. The rule, then, with such furniture is to bring it into a dry room, but not one which is unduly hot, and to leave it for as long as possible with all doors, drawers, etc. open.

Do not attempt to re-glue any failed joints whilst the wood is wet, because the glue will not hold properly. After being in the dry for some time, several weeks if possible, the job can be examined to see what attention it needs. This may involve dismantling, but do not take to pieces more than is essential. The individual faults can then be put right

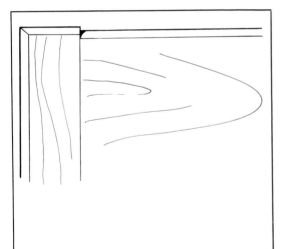

Fig. 1 Typical shrinkage of a clamped panel. Even after this movement the glue may still grip securely.

as outlined in other chapters. Polish is usually badly affected by damp, but even this may recover as the wood dries out. Try first rubbing with a reviver, using a warm rag, and working in a warm room. It will not respond, however, unless the dampness has been eliminated.

Furniture is seldom affected by dry rot unless it has been stored in a damp, unventilated cellar. Once badly attacked, however, it cannot be put right, because the substance of the wood itself has deteriorated. Dry rot usually belongs to the structure and fittings of the house itself, and invariably the treatment is drastic, involving the burning of all affected timber even beyond the parts obviously suffering. The fact that the dampness is stopped does not cause the dry rot to die out.

The furniture beetle

Furniture is liable to attack from the furniture beetle, especially old dry woodwork. Some woods are more liable to attack than others. Walnut in particular often suffers badly. On the other hand, mahogany seems immune. The only exception I have come across is that of a beech cabinet veneered with mahogany, in which the beetle had penetrated right through the veneer.

To understand the treatment it is desirable to know something of the pest and the cycle of its life. The eggs are laid in crevices, open joints, etc. The grubs are extremely small, and begin to burrow into the wood. They bite out channels, remaining in grub form for two years and occasionally more, when they burrow towards the surface and change into beetles, fully equipped with wings. They then bite their way through to the surface, and mate. The female lays eggs in likely places, cracks, open joints, and sometimes in old flight holes. These eggs hatch out, and the cycle starts all over again.

It is obvious from this that the holes in woodwork are the flight holes, and when they are discovered it is certain that the beetle has been at work in the substance of the wood for at least two years, perhaps longer, so that substantial damage has already been done to the wood. I was once called to repair a walnut bureau with cabriole legs. One of the latter had broken off at the ankle, and, although there were scarcely any signs on the surface, the whole foot could be crushed in the hand, as it was little more than a polished shell with scarcely any substance inside.

When wood is in this condition and has to bear strain (as a leg necessarily must) little can be done about it. When the piece is required for further everyday use the first obvious requirement is to try to stop further activity by the use of an insecticide, of which there are several on the market, but it is doubtful whether any one application is likely to be effective in so bad a case. If the grubs eat into any wood containing the insecticide they die, but the problem is to reach those at work in the depth of the wood. It helps if the liquid can be squirted into the holes, so that it may sponge its way in, but it is often impossible to reach right into the thickness.

What the repeated application of the insecticide does is to break the cycle of events. Thus, if rubbed all over surfaces, and in particular into crevices, any grubs beginning to attack the wood are poisoned. The same thing applies to the mature beetle on emerging at the surface. Since the period when the beetles emerge is in the late spring or early summer, it is at this time that special attention is needed. Often the presence of the pest can be detected by small piles of fine yellow dust. This often happens when the presence of the pest is otherwise unsuspected, and when they are found the item should be carefully examined for flight holes. The insecticide should be squirted into any such holes and over all other surfaces, especially open joints, etc., so that any grubs emerging from eggs and beginning to burrow are poisoned. Other furniture should also be treated because the beetle can fly and may land on other items and start the trouble. Some insecticides are available in aerosol containers which are useful in reaching difficult places, and the plastic container with injector is effective in forcing the liquid into the holes.

The presence of holes is not proof that the pest is still at work, but it is usually possible to detect recent holes by their appearance, the edges being sharp and the inside light yellow. Holes caused by an old colony which has died out are usually dark and often half-filled with furniture wax.

The above outlines the treatment for the arrest of the trouble, but takes no account of how far the structural strength has deteriorated. When the attack is only slight it is enough to treat with an insecticide, repeating the process periodically, and dealing with adjoining parts and other furniture, even though apparently unaffected. If, however, structural parts are in a bad way, the only plan is to replace them with sound wood, taking the precaution of rubbing the new wood with an insecticide. In the case of back rails and interior parts generally, this does not raise any great problem beyond those of the practical fitting.

However, suppose the item to be an antique and that the show wood has become affected. Clearly the first step is to stop further depredation, and generally this can only be done over a period of time. The question then arises, how far the job can be strengthened. It is only possible to consider each case individually. Such parts as rails can sometimes have a backing of sound wood applied to them, this being jointed or screwed to whatever adjoining members there may be, and glued on. This is often the case with, say, veneered parts which may be unmarked on the surface, but badly worm-eaten in the groundwork beneath.

When a part such as a leg is so badly attacked as to be liable to snap off, and the item is required for a further period of service, there is little to be done about it, short of the replacement of the affected part. This will probably call for the separating of the joints, and when there are four legs attached to rails forming a stand it usually entails separating at least one other leg. Sometimes it is possible to strain the rails sufficiently to enable tenons to be withdrawn, but it may be necessary to saw right through the tenon and fit a loose tenon or use dowels in their place. Treat all new parts with an insecticide.

It is possible to strengthen a part badly affected by immersing in glue size, allowing several hours for complete absorption to take place. It is then allowed to dry out completely. Another plan sometimes followed is to use a thinned-out solution of resin glue. Such parts can be strengthened by this treatment, but it is doubtful whether an item likely to be subjected to any great strain would be fit for everyday service. Sometimes it is possible to make a reasonably effective repair by cutting a groove at the back of a leg and letting in a sound strip of wood, see page 53.

Fumigation is effective in destroying the existing pest but it involves the use of a poisonous gas, and can only be used by firms equipped to deal with it. In any case, fumigation does not prevent future attack. Turps and paraffin are sometimes recommended, and they may kill some grubs, but both are volatile and once they have evaporated there is nothing to prevent continuance of the attack.

A point to note is that most insecticides are oil-based, and it is therefore a mistake to apply glue soon after treatment. Joints and any other parts to be glued should be treated and left for as long as possible before any glue is applied. One well-known manufacturer gives the following advice after the use of wood preservatives.

Most types of wood glues will give a satisfactory joint provided the general recommendations given below are followed.
1. After preservative treatment the treated wood should be allowed to dry thoroughly. This may take 3–5 days under warm, good drying conditions but longer if drying conditions are not ideal.
2. Surfaces to be glued should be roughened by light sanding to ensure maximum adhesion.
3. The recommendations of the manufacturers of the adhesives should be followed carefully.
Water-based glues of the type used for fixing posters or wallpaper, and some rubber-based adhesives used for upholstery, are unsuitable for treated wood.

Central heating

Many a collector knows to his cost that this can play havoc with old furniture. A piece may have stood in an old house since it was made and remained in good condition for years, and then has been moved to a house with central heating, or possibly the old house itself has had central heating installed. The inevitable has happened; panels have shrunk, joints opened, odd splits have occurred, and the clearance around doors and drawers has gaped.

The trouble is due to the dryness of the atmosphere, and to avoid it a humidifier should be installed. This is operated electrically, but it should be remembered that the water must be replaced periodically to counter the moisture lost by evaporation. Otherwise put an open vessel of water at the foot of the heat source.

Chapter fifteen

Renovating the Finish

Old furniture was finished in a variety of ways. Oak appears to have been varnished, painted or waxed. No doubt it was realized quite early on that, quite apart from appearance, some sort of finish was needed to seal the grain so that subsequent movement was minimized, and also to avoid the marking inevitable in everyday life. Table tops and other places where furniture was constantly handled, for instance, would rapidly be spoilt unless given some protective treatment. Oak, originally varnished, would subsequently be waxed. In the case of pieces coated with paint the latter has usually long since worn off or been stripped off, leaving a surface finished with wax. Sometimes one finds traces of paint in the recessed parts of carving, etc., but it would be a mistake to assume that paint was necessarily the original finish because later generations unashamedly may have painted over the oak to give a bright appearance. I have known trade cases where paint has been deliberately applied, a piece of panelling being painted green, allowed to harden, then stripped off, the result being a faded greenish tinge over the whole.

The probability is that walnut was originally varnished in several coats, each being rubbed down after drying intervals, and finally waxed. Mahogany of the eighteenth century was frequently varnished after rubbing with linseed oil, though Sheraton in his *Cabinet Dictionary* says that mahogany was finished with linseed oil and rubbed with a mixture of linseed oil and brickdust.

This use of oil raises an interesting point. Some old mahogany is of a pronounced reddish shade, whereas other pieces are of a more golden, honey colour. It is not merely a question of the particular species of wood. Early mahogany up to about the 1760s or '70s was of the dark Cuban variety and, except for a certain amount of fading, remains much as it was originally. Towards the end of the century, however, mahogany from Honduras was used, a lighter wood, and it is this that may vary in colour. My own theory is that the difference was caused by the original oiling before subsequent varnishing, oiling, polishing or waxing. In some cases alkanet root was used with the oil. The root of the plant, in appearance much like any other root and anything from about 6mm.–12·5mm. ($\frac{1}{4}$in.–$\frac{1}{2}$in.) or so in diameter, was beaten with a hammer into shreds and steeped in the linseed oil, which in time turned

Fig. 1 Chest of drawers awaiting finishing after repairs are completed.

to a reddish shade. The redness of the mahogany was thus emphasized, and I suspect that this was the cause of the colour found in most old mahogany. On the other hand, the honey colour so prized today was, I think, originally oiled with plain linseed oil, no alkanet root being used.

French or shellac polishing appears to have been introduced in the early years of the nineteenth century, and it brought into being an entirely new trade, that of the polisher. It is a highly skilled process, the polish being applied with a rubber rather than with a brush, and obtaining its effect by the friction of the smooth rubber over the semi-hard previous coat. At best it has a fine, lustrous effect which appears to be the burnishing of the wood surface rather than an applied finish. A drawback is that it is not heat-proof, and is easily marked by hot plates, hot water, spirits, etc.

Such finishes as cellulose, poly-urethane, etc. can be ruled out because they belong to the present century, though the possibility of their having been used over an existing finish has to be taken into account. The following tests for kinds of finish can be applied to a small, unnoticeable part of the work.

Since all finishes are liable to have been subsequently waxed, however, this should be got rid of first by rubbing with turps. If methylated spirit is rubbed over the surface the finish will soften slowly if it is French polish, whereas oil varnish, cellulose and other modern finishes will not be affected. If scraped with a knife French polish will produce a thin shaving which breaks up easily; oil varnish will give a much stronger shaving; but cellulose will merely form a whitish dust. The application of acetone will soften French polish, oil varnish and cellulose, but have no effect on a plastic varnish.

The immediate question that confronts the restorer is the treatment to be given to a piece of furniture, the condition of which may vary from that of having become merely dull to an item which has been repaired and has several replacement parts. It can generally be taken that the less drastic the treatment the better (and certainly the safer) it is. It may take longer and call for a good deal of elbow grease, but it is worth it. Occasionally, however, it happens that there is no option. I have seen cases where a fine mahogany chest of drawers has at some time been given a coat of thick oil varnish or, even worse, of varnish stain. It has an unmistakable look: cheap, glittery and sticky. Nothing can be done with it; it has to be stripped off, and if in the process the original finish comes with it, it cannot be helped. In any case, it is better than using the steel scraper which will leave the surface just like any other piece of new wood. Various strippers are available, but it is better to choose one of the non-caustic types as this is free from any darkening tendency.

Some strippers need to be left on for some time, others need attention as soon as the finish softens because the latter tends to harden again as the liquid dries out, and sometimes this is quite volatile. However, the instructions given on the container should be followed. Sometimes rag is effective in removing the soft finish, but often a piece of hard wood with square edge is useful. Alternatively, fine steel wool is helpful in removing it. Any dents, scratches, etc. remain and these are left unless really bad. It will probably be found that this stripping leaves a smooth surface with the open grain filled in, and this can be finished with wax. If, however, the item is liable to be subjected to much handling it is a good plan to give one or two rubbers of French polish. This will help to keep out dirt and build up a slight preliminary shine. Wax polish follows when the surface is hard.

Fortunately most antiques have escaped this fate and cleaning is the first necessity. Ordinary soap will usually do this, warm water and rag being used. Do not flood on water, and wipe dry as soon as possible. If this is not effective, a mixture of turps and linseed oil will often shift grease and dirt. In fact, it is generally best to use this first and then soapy water afterwards, as this removes any greasiness in the oil and turps.

In the trade ordinary household soda dissolved in warm water is used for cleaning, but only a very weak solution must be used because too strong a cleaner will strip off old polish or varnish as well as dirt. All traces of soda must be wiped off afterwards to prevent further action.

Other alternatives that can be tried are water and vinegar, paraffin and soapy water. The latter must be shaken up frequently as the one is merely held in suspension in the other. Sometimes merely rubbing with wax polish is an effective cleanser, the turps being the active agent.

An excellent cleanser and one which revives old polish at the same time is the following. Boil 0·568 litre (1 pint) of distilled water and add to it 114gm. ($\frac{1}{4}$lb.) castile soap powder. Let the soap powder dissolve completely. In a separate tin pour 0·568 litre (1 pint) of best American turps and add to it 57gm. (2oz.) of best beeswax and 57gm. (2oz.) of white paraffin wax. Heat these by putting the tin in a basin of boiling water—do not heat over a flame. When the wax has completely dissolved, shoot the whole into the distilled water and allow to cool. After twenty-four hours it will be ready for use. Always stir up thoroughly first. If castile soap powder cannot be obtained shred a cake of any good quality soap. If American turps is not available, turps substitute will have to be used.

When a piece has been repaired there are inevitably some new parts, and it is advisable to colour these first and fix them before water or turps from the cleaner gets to them. Various stains are available, but an invaluable substance is Vandyke crystals dissolved in hot water and allowed to cool. The mixture should be made up really thick, almost a paste, and a little Scotch glue added. Immediately before use some ·880 ammonia (P) is poured in and the mixture brushed on to the wood and immediately rubbed with a coarse cloth until dry (P after a substance denotes that it is poisonous). Alternatively, a boot brush can be used. If too dark, it can be lightened or removed entirely with water. It can be used for oak, and is also suitable for the colder shades of mahogany, but if a redder tone is needed, bichromate of potash (P) can be substituted, or a mixture of this and the Vandyke crystals can be used. Walnut seldom needs darkening, but a weak solution of the Vandyke mixture can be used if necessary. Sometimes a bleach may be needed.

An attractive brown shade in oak can also be produced with ordinary household soda. Its degree of darkening depends upon the strength of the mixture. It has the curious effect of turning the figure or rays darker than the rest of the wood, whereas they are normally lighter. The wood must be washed afterwards to get rid of all traces of soda, otherwise it may attack any finish subsequently applied. Soda can also be used for

mahogany which it will deepen considerably. However, as quite a lot of moisture is used in the process it is not advisable to use it on a veneered surface—at any rate when Scotch glue has been used.

It will be realized that a certain amount of experiment is needed to ascertain the strength of the stain, and considerable dilution may be necessary. Remember that bichromate, when dissolved in water, forms a liquid of bright orange colour, but this has no connection with the darkening it produces in the mahogany, as its effect is purely chemical, and the full effect is only realized as the wood dries out. It is, therefore, advisable to try out the effect on a spare piece of the same kind of wood. Some varieties of mahogany are much more readily affected than others. Some woods, pine for instance, do not react to the bichromate. Oak is slightly darkened by it, but may have a slightly greenish hue or reddish shade according to species.

Ammonia (P) is an excellent darkening agent for oak. It can be brush-applied. Sometimes a mixture of ammonia and bichromate is effective, but remember that the full darkening is not complete until the wood has dried out. It is also as well to keep in mind that some varieties of oak are more readily affected than others.

To any of these mixtures a little powder pigment can be added to vary the colour, but is should be used sparingly because too much gives a cloudy effect. Sometimes strong permanganate of potash (P) is used, but the colour is fugitive and when a patch has to be matched to the surrounding wood it may eventually fade to a qu te different colour.

Having stained any patches or new parts to match the old, a protective rubber of French polish should be applied. It will be realized that the new parts and patches are necessarily raw, yet have to be made to match the surrounding parts which have had years of polishing with wax. It would be impossible to build up a finish purely with wax in so short a time. Consequently the grain is filled and a basic shine built up with the French polishing rubber. The filler can be a proprietary paste such as Wheeler's compound or plaster of Paris tinted with a dry pigment. The coloured plaster is picked up with a damp rag and rubbed across the grain. When hard after twelve hours or more the parts are wiped over with linseed oil which will kill any whiteness left in the filler, and left to harden. Several rubbers of French polish follow with drying intervals until the patches approximate to the rest of the job. If the colour appears too light it can be darkened with French polish, tinted with a little lamp black, and burnt umber powder pigment applied with a small pencil brush. This again is left to harden and fixed with a further rubber of French polish lightly applied. Again, do not overdo the powder pigment because it tends to cloud the grain.

It is inevitable that the rubber will stray to an extent over the surrounding surface. If the surface has not been cleaned, it should be wiped over with methylated spirit to remove any trace of wax because French polish will flake if applied over wax.

A substance I have found useful to produce a faded look to walnut, and sometimes mahogany, is green copperas (ferrous sulphate) (**P**) dissolved in water. The strength of the mixture is found by experiment. If too strong it will turn the wood to an Air Force blue. Its effect becomes apparent only as it dries out, so start off with a weak solution.

We now have to consider the case of a surface in a really bad way. Possibly a reviver has failed to have any effect, and quite likely the piece has been French polished at some time and the polish has crazed or perished. There is only one answer. It has to be stripped off. A non-caustic proprietary stripper should be used (caustic strippers are liable to darken the wood). The general procedure described on page 114 and the instructions on the container should be followed.

Faults

Scratches. The treatment depends upon how deep they are. If they do not penetrate through the film of polish they can be eased down with flour grade glasspaper first dipped into linseed oil. It may be that this will take some of the colour out of the work if the original polish had colour in it. If this is the case, a rubber or two of dark polish will have to be given locally over the the rubbed-down area. Usually garnet polish will do the trick, but if necessary it can be made darker with a little spirit

aniline dye (**P**). The latter is made up separately and a little added to the polish. It is usually necessary afterwards to polish over the entire surface with clear polish, and then wax.

Deeper scratches cannot be dealt with in this way, and filling with coloured wax is the only answer. Dry pigment is mixed with beeswax whilst molten. When cold, the wax is rubbed across the scratch to fill in. In winter time it often helps to *slightly* warm the wax to soften it, but avoid surplus wax on the surface as far as possible. Afterwards the whole is rubbed level with fine glasspaper. Sometimes a rag rubbed vigorously across the scratch will do the trick, the generated heat helping matters.

It may be possible to fill in medium scratches with polish applied with a finely pointed brush. The difficulty comes in levelling afterwards because the polish is bound to build up somewhat at each side. Levelling with fine glasspaper and oil when thoroughly hard is the only way, after which the whole is re-polished.

Small scratches which show white can often be made less noticeable by rubbing the exposed face of a broken brazil nut across them, the oil in the nut exuding.

Cracks. When these are large they should be filled in with slivers of wood as described, Chapter three. Narrow ones are filled with coloured wax in the way already described, except that the wider part of a crack may need the wax melting into it. The usual way is to heat a pointed metal rod, hold it over the crack, and press the coloured wax against it so that the latter runs down. Afterwards level with chisel and finish with fine glasspaper.

Bruises. In bare wood these can often be taken out by putting a damp cloth over the part and placing a hot iron over it. This is of little value on an unbroken polished surface as the damp cannot penetrate. Sometimes pricking the surface and using the damp rag and hot iron is effective, the moisture entering the prick holes. As a result there may be further damage due to the deterioration of the polish under the damp heat, and it may be better to leave the bruise untouched. Filling with wax is usually of little value owing to its liability to fall out. If it is done, the bottom of the bruise should be scored to provide a key.

Heat and water marks. Such marks are caused by a hot plate, or by hot water being spilt. Try rubbing with equal quantities of linseed oil and turps applied with a warm rag. Alternatively, try camphorated oil (**P**). Remove the oil by rubbing with vinegar. Several applications may be needed.

Glass marks. These are caused by a glass, damp with spirits, being placed on the table. Sometimes it is left until the softened polish hardens so that when the glass is lifted it pulls the polish away with it. Alternatively, it is rubbed before the spirit-softened polish has a chance to harden, and the polish is lifted. The place needs to be coloured as a rule, coloured polish being applied in short strokes in the direction of the grain. It is then built up level with the general surface, polish being applied with the brush. When completely hard it is rubbed with flour glasspaper dipped into linseed oil, and the whole surface worked over with the rubber.

Ink marks. The use of a household bleach such as *Domestos* will often remove these, the liquid being applied with a fine brush over the area only. Wash off immediately the mark has been taken out. Failing this, diluted nitric acid (**P**) can be used. This may tend to turn the mark white, and it is then wiped with camphorated oil (**P**).

White flecks in the grain. These in French polished work are due to plaster of Paris having been used as a filler without the wood having been first sealed with two rubbers of polish, or possibly to no colouring having been added to the filler. It is difficult to correct because the polish covers the filler. The only way short of stripping is to rub down with glasspaper and use linseed oil. It is not likely to be effective until the polish has been penetrated.

Soft polish. Sometimes one comes across a relatively new item or an old one which has been re-polished in which the polish is not really hard so that an item left upon it leaves a mark. It is due to the use of a faulty polish which contains a gum which never really hardens, or to poor shellac. White polish in particular may suffer from the defect. No cure is possible; the whole has to be stripped off and the work re-polished.

Materials used in renovations

French polishes. Obtain ready-made of reliable make.
White. Milky white for light wood. Do not use on dark wood.
Transparent. Water clear. Retains natural colour of wood.
Button. Yellow tint, slightly opaque. Do not use on dark stain, or after dark polish.
Orange. Golden brown colour.
Garnet. Dark brown shade.
Black. For ebonised wood.
Coloured. Polish for matching and tinting. Add spirit-soluble aniline dye (**P**) to white, transparent or orange polish as required.

Poly-urethane polishes. Water and heat resistant. Used chiefly for table tops, etc. Some require addition of catalyst. Follow instructions on container.

Table top polishes. Cellulose-based, and considerably resistant to water and light heat marking.

Wax polishes.
Normal. Shred yellow or brown beeswax and dissolve in turps. Process can be speeded by heating in basin of hot water (do not use a naked flame). A little Carnauba dissolved separately and added to normal wax hardens the whole. Many proprietary wax polishes are also available.
Antique. Add lamp black powder pigment to the molten normal polish. Mix thoroughly.
White. Add zinc white powder pigment to normal polish. Used in limed finish.

Revivers
1 part raw linseed oil, 1 part vinegar, or
1 part raw linseed oil, 1 part vinegar, 1 part methylated spirit. Other revivers are on pages 114–115.

Darkening agents

Oak. Vandyke crystals dissolved in warm water to a thick paste. Strain through muslin and add a little ·880 ammonia (**P**) immediately before use. Gives cold brown shade and is the basis of most oak water stains. To warm the shade make up separately a little red stain with eosin powder and add sparingly to the basic Vandyke. A spoonful of Scotch glue is often helpful, but this will keep only a few days. See its use described on page 115.

Ammonia (**P**) also tends to darken oak, but is more generally used for fuming, the work being placed in a closed cupboard with one or two saucerfuls of ·880 ammonia. Keep ammonia from fingers as it turns them yellow and is painful. Fumes should be avoided as they are powerful.

Asphaltum dissolved in turpentine also gives a rich brown shade and does not raise the grain. Heat glue-kettle fashion, not with a naked flame—strain through muslin and add a little gold size to act as a binder. Household soda dissolved in water darkens both oak and mahogany. Turns the rays of oak a dark shade (see page 115).

Mahogany. Universal stain is bichromate of potash (**P**) dissolved in water to a saturated solution and diluted as required. It also darkens oak, but has no effect on most softwoods. See also use of Vandyke crystals, soda, etc.

Aniline dyes (**P**) dissolved in water or turps according to type can also be used. Vandyke brown for oak. Bismarck brown is a fiery-red colour and warms the tone, but must be used sparingly as it is powerful.

Ebony. Use aniline black, water, oil or spirit, following with black polish.

Harewood (grey). Dissolve green copperas (sulphate of iron) (**P**) in water. Try effect and dilute if necessary. Effect apparent only as liquid dries.

Filler. Plaster of Paris tinted with powder pigment (burn umber for oak, and red ochre for mahogany) often used. When hard it is coated with linseed oil to kill whiteness, and surplus wiped off (see also page 117). Before use the work should have received two coats of French polish, otherwise the plaster may later turn white in the grain.

Alternatively, use a paste filler such as Wheeler's compound, available in various shades or neutral.

Stopping. For filling nail holes and other blemishes. Beaumontage is often used. Mix equal parts beeswax and rosin, and add a few flakes of shellac. Melt in a tin, and add powder colour as required, burnt umber for dark oak, red ochre for mahogany, or a mixture of colours. Stick stopping is also available ready-made. Melted into hole and levelled.

Strippers. Use a proprietary non-caustic type. Get rid of all traces of stripper before applying any other finish. Follow instructions on container.

Bleaches. Mild bleaching can be done with oxalic acid (**P**) dissolved in water. For any serious lightening of colour use one of the proprietary bleaches. These are effective in lightening the tone on some woods, but will not affect any stain which may have been used.

Lubricants. For moving parts of woodwork (drawers, etc.) use candlegrease rubbed cold on to the surface.

General materials

Carbon tetrachloride (**P**). Used to de-grease wood of a greasy nature before gluing, notably teak and rosewood.

Crocus powder. Fine, abrasive powder lightly dusted over polished surface to dull down. Also used as dressing for a strop used for carving tools. Mix the powder with oil or vaseline.

Glossary

Bubble. A small area of veneer which has lost adhesion with the groundwork and has lifted. It is usually necessary to cut through the veneer with a thin knife, following the grain direction, to enable fresh glue to be inserted. It is afterwards cramped down with a flat block with newspaper interposed.

Burnisher, chain. Sometimes used to round over the edges, etc. to simulate the effects of wear (see page 16).

Caul. A flat panel of wood, sometimes faced with zinc, used in pressing down veneer. It should be slightly larger than the area to be veneered and must be free from surface depressions and similar blemishes. If it has to be jointed to make up the width the joint should be assembled with resin glue, or the back reinforced with cross-battens. Otherwise when heated the joints may separate.

Clamped panel. A fairly wide panel strengthened across the grain with end pieces (clamps) tongued and grooved on. Bureau falls were often made in this way (see page 79).

Cocked bead. A small bead, usually about 3mm. ($\frac{1}{8}$in.) wide, applied to the edges and standing proud of the surface. Often fitted around drawers and sometimes doors (see page 68).

Contact adhesive. A rubber-based adhesive sometimes used for repairs which would be awkward to cramp. It is applied to both parts and allowed to become touch dry. When the two are brought together the grab is immediate (see page 109).

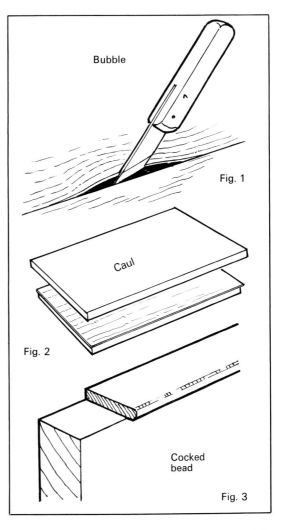

Bubble

Fig. 1

Caul

Fig. 2

Cocked bead

Fig. 3

Counterboring. When a part such as a top has to be fixed with screws driven through a wide rail it is simpler to recess the screw head deeply by counter-boring and use relatively short screws as shown. Note that the large counterbore hole must be bored first otherwise there is no centre on which the point of the bit can be started. Fig. 4.

Countersinking. The recessing of a screw head flush with or slightly below the surface of the wood, Fig. 5A. Snail countersink is used, C. In some cases screw cups are fitted, and these may be of either the raised type, D, for use with raised head screws, or the flush type, E, for normal countersunk screws. Fig. 5.

Counter veneering. The laying of two sheets of veneer on each side of the groundwork. The advantage is that it helps to keep the latter stable and in any case strengthens the whole. The inner or counter-veneer has its grain at right angles with that of the groundwork, and the face veneer in line with it. Both sides have the same treatment so that the pull is equalized, Fig. 6.

Cross-banding. The use of a veneered strip around the edges of a panel, table top, etc., the grain running crosswise. Usually the whole top is veneered, but sometimes it is solid with a shallow rebate worked around the edges to take the veneer. Frequently inlay lines or strings are used at each side of the cross-banding, C. In the Queen Anne walnut period the cross-banding was frequently, although not invariably, butted at the corners as at B, but the tendency in later periods was to mitre the corners as at A, Fig. 7.

Cross-bearers. Made in pairs and used in pressing down the caul in veneered work. The inner edges are slightly rounded in their length so that when cramps are put on at the ends the pressure is applied at the centre first, thus squeezing the glue outwards. For the same reason when three or more pairs of cross-bearers are used the centre ones are cramped first, Fig. 8.

Dovetailed key. Sometimes used in repair work across a crack in a panel to strengthen it. It is invariably fitted at the back (see page 85).

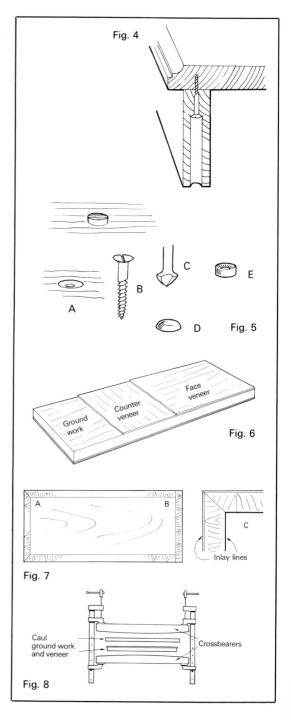

Fig. 4

Fig. 5

Fig. 6

Fig. 7

Fig. 8

Ear pieces. Term used for projecting pieces applied at each side of a cabriole leg, Fig. 9.

Fielding. Treatment of a panel in which the edges have a broad, sloping chamfer, giving the effect of a raised panel. In old work a special fielding plane was sometimes used, but more generally the chamfer was worked with the badger plane. The width of the chamfer was cut in with the cutting gauge and a square rebate planed first, the chamfering following. In all cases the cross-grain sides were planed first so that any splitting out was removed when the edges with the grain were dealt with. Sometimes a small hollow moulding was worked as in example B, Fig. 10.

Glue blocks. Blocks from 25mm.–50mm. (1in.–2in.) long and about 21mm. or 32mm. ($\frac{7}{8}$in. or 1$\frac{1}{4}$in.) section, used to strengthen joints, etc. Two adjacent faces are at right angles and the extreme corner taken off. The diagonally-opposite corner is chamfered. When fixing the two faces are glued and the block rubbed back and forth two or three times to squeeze out surplus glue and bring the faces into close contact. Unless the extreme corner is removed the two faces may not bed down on the surfaces. When the parts meet at an odd angle the blocks must be planed accordingly, Fig. 11.

Humidifier. An electrically-operated device to counter the dryness of central-heating.

Jubilee clip. A metal band-clip tightened by a screw. Often useful to tighten the cracked end of a turning when being glued, and to prevent further splitting when boring, Fig. 12.

Kerf. The cut by the saw in wood. It may be wide or narrow according to the thickness of the saw blade, and the amount of set it has.

Lapped drawer. One which projects from the face of the carcase and with a moulding around the edges, thus forming a rebate all round. The effect is partly decorative, but it also serves to make the drawer dust-proof (see page 70).

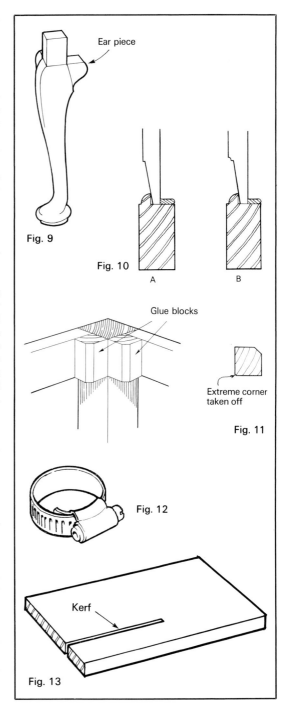

Ear piece

Fig. 9

Fig. 10

A

B

Glue blocks

Extreme corner taken off

Fig. 11

Fig. 12

Kerf

Fig. 13

Line, inlay. Narrow strip of boxwood, ebony or other fine wood used in inlaying. Also called a string.

Loose-leaf gold. Leaves of gold which are free from backing. Sold in thin paper 'books', twenty-five leaves to a book. Used in both water and oil gilding. (See also transfer gold.)

Loose tenon. A separate tenon glued into a notch cut to receive it. It is sometimes needed when a tenon has snapped off. It may occupy the full width of the wood, or be stopped at the top.

Pelleting. A method of filling-in screw and other holes with wood. The grain of the pellet must be in the same direction as that of the wood into which it is recessed. Dowel rod is useless because the grain direction is wrong and is eventually left standing proud of the surface, apart from looking wrong. The pellets are turned in lengths of about 102mm. (4in.), the grain running crosswise, as shown. It is not possible to turn in much greater length as the wood is liable to snap. The pellets are separated, glued, and tapped into the holes, the tops being left proud and levelled after glue has set.

Pocket screwing. Used widely for fixing table and other tops to frames having deep rails or solid ends. A hole is bored at a slight angle downwards from the top edge, and a sloping recess cut with a gouge at the inside to meet the hole, enabling the screw to go in flush as shown, Fig. 16.

Pot life. The length of time a glue remains usable after preparation. When the hardener of resin glue is added to the glue the pot life is from hour to hour according to temperature.

Pressure-sensitive tape. Paper tape coated with adhesive on one side. It sticks only when pressed into position. Useful to hold parts in position when gluing repairs (see also page 59) Fig. 17.

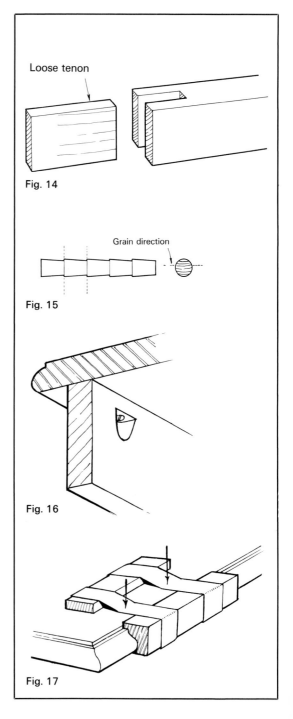

Loose tenon

Fig. 14

Grain direction

Fig. 15

Fig. 16

Fig. 17

Rubbed joint. One in which there is no additional strengthening such as dowels or tongues. The parts are planed to a close fit, the one piece placed in the bench vice and the other turned upside down and placed alongside. The two are glued in a single operation and the one immediately erected on the other. It is then rubbed back and forth two or three times to bring the two into close contact and to squeeze out surplus glue. Normally used only for Scotch glue, as other adhesives have no immediate tackiness.

Rule joint. A mechanical joint used on some table tops and sometimes on doors. In a table the main top is rounded and the leaf hollowed. The metal hinge has its knuckle on the reverse side from the countersinking of the screw holes (see page 98).

Sandbag. A canvas bag filled with fine sand used to press down veneer over a shaped groundwork. A sand box is used for similar purpose but is an open-topped box containing sand. When Scotch glue is used the sandbag must be heated.

Shaper. Tool having similar uses to that of a file but with open slots between the teeth so that it never clogs (see page 16).

Shelf life. The period in which an adhesive can remain unused after manufacture before deterioration sets in. Refers in particular to resin glues which, when in syrup form, may remain in good condition for three to six months. When in powder form the shelf life is from one to two years.

Sliver or shiver. A thin strip of wood of slightly tapered section to fill in splits or open joints, Fig. 20. When the split runs away to nothing it is usually necessary to open it somewhat by inserting the end of the tenon saw and working it up and down. Otherwise the sliver cannot be inserted. It is glued in, care being taken to see that the wood at each side is level. It is levelled after the glue has set (see also page 26).

Softening blocks. Used beneath cramp shoes to prevent marking of the surface. They are oddments of wood, and may be simple square pieces, or specially shaped to suit the work.

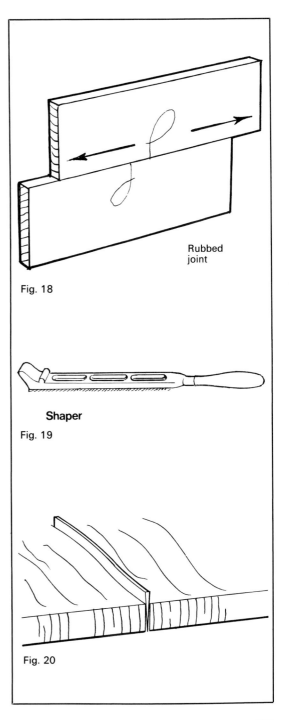

Rubbed joint

Fig. 18

Shaper

Fig. 19

Fig. 20

Spigot. A projecting piece or dowel at the end of a turning engaging with a corresponding hole in another piece of turning (see page 51).

Squaring rod or diagonal strip. A rod or lath pointed at one end used to test the squareness of a cabinet carcase. Placed diagonally across the carcase and the length noted with pencil. When reversed into the opposite corners the same length will register if the carcase is square (see page 20).

String, inlay. See Line.

Stuck moulding. This is one worked in the solid, A, as distinct from being applied, B. The latter is usually the cheaper method in that the moulding can be obtained in length and be mitred round, and complications in the joints avoided. Sometimes for practical reasons there may be no option but to apply it. An example of this is a bolection moulding, C, which would be too complicated to stick as the joints would be extremely awkward to cut, (Fig. 22).

Tambour. A sliding door or cover composed of a series of strips, plain or moulded, glued to a canvas backing and capable of sliding around a curve. It may move vertically or horizontally, according to position, Fig. 23.

Tooling wheel. Solid brass wheel with pattern embossed around the periphery used to emboss leather (see page 86).

Tourniquet. Length of cord or string looped around two parts of a job with centre stick which is revolved, so pulling the parts together (see page 28).

Transfer gold. Similar to loose-leaf gold (q.v.), but each leaf is attached to tissue paper by a film of wax. The leaves can be handled and pressed on with the fingers. Used in oil gilding.

Winding. Term used to describe a carcase or framework, the two corresponding sides of which are not in the same plane. If the item is true it is said to be 'free of wind'.

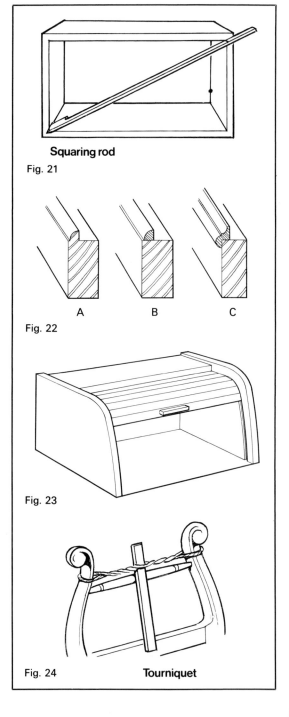

Squaring rod

Fig. 21

Fig. 22

Fig. 23

Fig. 24   Tourniquet

Index